# The Power of the Seed

## Releasing Supernatural Harvest Into Your Life

Daniel King

*The Power of the Seed:*
*Releasing Supernatural Harvest Into Your Life*

ISBN:1-931810-02-8


Daniel King
King Ministries
PO Box 701113
Tulsa, OK 74170-1113 USA
1-877-431-4276
daniel@kingministries.com

# Introduction

Dear Friend,

The seed contains the greatest power in the universe. A tiny seed, planted into the ground, will produce a massive harvest. All life on earth depends upon the miracle of seed-growth.

The seed reflects God's miracle nature. Throughout the Bible, God chose to use the example of seedtime and harvest as a metaphor for giving and receiving. The miracle you need depends upon your understanding of the power of the seed.

In this book are over three hundred keys to understanding the power of the seed. They are arranged in order from Genesis to Revelation, thus providing a complete overview of what the Bible says about giving.

If you need a miracle, you can use these principles to activate God's power in your life. If you are a pastor, you can use this material in your offering sermons each week for the next five years.

Allow this book to build your faith as you believe for your harvest.

Always sowing,

Daniel King

P.S. This book is my seed into your life. I am praying that as you read, unprecedented harvest will be released into your finances, your health, your family, and your spiritual walk with God. Get ready to receive your miracle!

*Why should you read the Power of the Seed?*

Discoveries Decide Your Seasons. Discoveries Decide Your Significance. This explains the remarkable impact of the life and ministry of Daniel King. His rare *humility* has birthed uncommon hunger for wisdom. His *hunger* for wisdom is truly setting him apart and making him a true magnet for the miraculous. The keen spiritual sensitivity of Daniel King has made him an extraordinary Instrument in the hands of God. His obsession to *heal the broken* has opened more doors than he will ever be able to fill. His newest work, *The Power of The Seed,* could breathe new life into the Body of Christ. I predict that it will Unleash a new wave of miracles beyond your own imagination. When you think you have read it all....read Daniel King. His heart is aflame for God...and His mind has captured the hidden mysteries that every child of God longs to understand. I commend this newest work to every believer who is serious about living a truly *Uncommon* Life.

**- Mike Murdock, The Wisdom Center**

I believe the book you hold in your hands, *The Power Of The Seed*, is a valuable tool in being able to transform your life. As I read it, I was impressed with the understanding that Daniel has on this subject. It is refreshing to see younger men grasp these principles to set the body of Christ free from the spirit of poverty. It will be a great blessing to all those who embrace these principles. **- Robb Thompson, Family Harvest Church**

*The Power of the Seed* by Daniel King uses a very interesting approach to Seedtime and harvest. No other book on the subject brings the reader so many organized streams of information about the Seed. Daniel literally takes you from one end of the Bible to the other, and from one Bible hero to the next, never leaving the subject of the power of the Seed until he has given you 324 separate secrets about the Seed. The Book is an interesting read as well as being a great text book on the Seed, one that you will keep and use over and over again. **- John Avanzini, The Debt-Free Army**

This book is just out of this world! I don't know how many copies of *The Power of the Seed*, I have given away or told people to get. I travel with this book because I like it so much. Daniel goes from Genesis to Revelation showing everything the Bible says about the power of the seed. How can you have a harvest if you don't sow seed? **- Marilyn Hickey, Marilyn Hickey Ministries**

# Secrets of the Seed from Creation

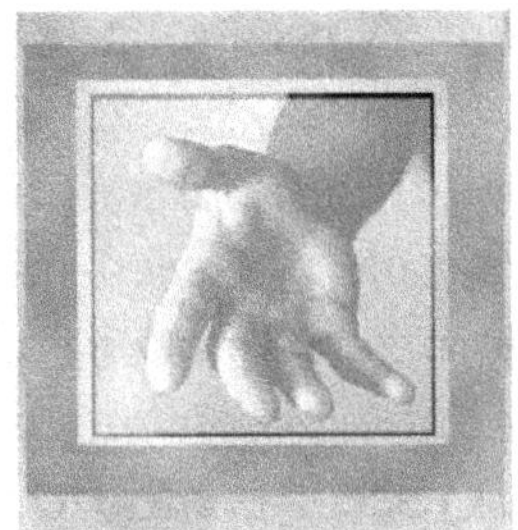

**1. God is a Seed-Sower!**

In the beginning of time, when God wanted a friend, He personally created the entire universe as a gift to Adam. This world is the gift that keeps on giving. The air you breathe, and the plants that give you food, and the sun that warms you are just as much God's gifts to you as they were to Adam. Before you were born, He gave you far more than you can ever hope to repay.

The most meaningful gifts I have ever received at Christmas time have been handmade projects. In contrast to generic storebought gifts, these personal creations have lasting sentimental value. God gave the ultimate creative gift. With great care, He carved out mountains and valleys, scattered the stars in the sky, and gave life to birds that fly, fish that swim, and animals of every variety. Could there be a better gift? The world around us is proof that God is the ultimate Seed-Sower.

**2. God gives first in every relationship.**

In God's first interaction with mankind, He postured Himself as a giver. God created a gift before there was anyone to give it to. First He created the world, then He created someone to give it to. The first action God took in His relationship with Adam was to give him the world. God sowed the seed of His creation hoping for the harvest of a relationship with Adam.

In respect to your life, God always plants the first seed in His hope for the harvest of a relationship with you. *"But God demonstrates His own love for us in this: While we were still sinners, Christ died for us"* (Romans 5:8). Before you were worthy to have a relationship with God, He planted the precious seed of His only Son thus making it possible for you to enter into a relationship.

**3. Seeds are God's building blocks of life.**

The creation miracle is a seed-miracle! *"God said, 'Let the land produce vegetation: seed-bearing plants and trees on the land that bear fruit with seed in it, according to their various kinds.' And it was so"* (Genesis 1:11). Seeds are the mechanisms which guarantee the continuance of God's creation. Without seeds, creation would

**Proof that God is a Giver**

* God said to Adam, "**I give**..." (Genesis 1:29) and again "...**I give**..." (Genesis 1:30).
* "God so loved that **He gave**..." (John 3:16).
* "Your Father has been pleased **to give** you the kingdom" (Luke 12:32).
* "We have [received] the Spirit who is from God, that we may understand what **God has freely given** us" (1 Corinthians 2:12).
* "He that spared not His own Son, but delivered Him up for us all, how shall He not with Him also **freely give us** all things?" (Romans 8:32 - KJV).
* "...The Son of Man did not come to be served, but to serve, and **to give** His life as a ransom for many" (Matthew 20:28).

have been a short-lived party since all the plants would have withered and died. God is a Seed-Sower and He embedded His essence into creation. All of nature reflects God's nature by continuing the process of sowing and reaping.

**4. Increase is God's mandate for all living creatures.**

*"God blessed [the fish and birds] and said, 'Be fruitful and increase in number...'"* (Genesis 1:22). This "Blessing of Increase" is the first blessing in the Bible. Fruitfulness, growth, harvest, increase, and multiplication are the direct results of God's blessings.

**5. Seasons are essential to the process of sowing and reaping.**

God created the seasons for a specific reason. *"...God said, 'Let there be lights in the expanse of the sky to separate the day from the night, and let them serve as signs to mark seasons and days and years, and let them be lights in the expanse of the sky to give light on the earth.' And it was so."* (Genesis 1:14-15). The seasons of life are governed by God. He created the seasons so there would be a separation between the time of sowing, the time of growing, and the time of reaping. All three seasons are essential parts of life. Hours, days, weeks, months, and years of waiting between seasons give us time to show our trust in God.

God always waits for the right season before moving. *"... when the fullness of the time was come, God sent forth His Son..."* (Galatians 4:4 -KJV). This verse could be rendered, "when the season was exactly right, God planted His Seed."

**6. Seed-sowing is a law God set in motion in the beginning.**

*"...God said, 'Let the land produce vegetation: seed-bearing plants and trees on the land that bear fruit with seed in it, according to their various kinds.' And it was so. The land produced vegetation: plants bearing seed according to their kinds and trees bearing fruit with seed in it according to their kinds. And God saw that it was good"* (Genesis 1:11-12).

The power of the seed guarantees the continuance of God's creation. If seeds stopped producing harvests, every plant, animal, and human being would be extinct in one generation. If God wanted the whole world to be destroyed, He would not have to send a fireball, all He would have to do is stop the ability of seeds to grow.

**7. Both God's creation and God's kingdom operate on the principles of the seed.**

God created both physical and spiritual laws to govern the universe. The law of gravity keeps us attached to the ground and the law of sowing and reaping keeps us from starving. Every physical law has a spiritual parallel.

The spiritual law of seedtime and harvest is as absolute as the physical law of gravity. The law of gravity states that "what goes UP must come DOWN." The law of seedtime and harvest is equally valid. It states: "What goes DOWN (into the ground) must come UP (as a harvest)."

**8. You will only reap that which you sow.**

*"God said, 'Let the land produce vegetation: seed-bearing plants and trees on the land that bear fruit with seed in it,* ***each according to its own kind****' And it was so."* (Genesis 1:11 - Own translation). Everything reproduces after its own kind. Corn seed grows corn stalks. Apple seed grows apple trees. No farmer plants an orange seed and expects a pear tree to grow.

The seed you plant will be the seed that grows. *"Do not be deceived: God cannot be mocked. A man reaps what he sows"* (Galatians 6:7). This can be a little scary if we have been planting bad seed. Why are dads so protective of their teenage daughters? Because they do not want their daughters to date any boys who were like them when they were teenagers.

**9. Whatever you have a need of, plant a seed of.**

If you want love, give someone love. If you desire joy in your life, plant some joy. (The act of giving joy will make you joyful.) If you want a financial harvest, then plant a financial seed. If you want someone to be your friend, be a friend to someone else.

This is what I call the Universal Law of the Mirror. Life is like a mirror. If you frown in the mirror, the guy you are looking at is going to frown right back at you. If you smile in the mirror of life, everyone you see is going to smile at you. Life will treat you the way you treat life.

Every seed you plant will be multiplied back into your life. This verse illustrates this concept. *"Do not judge, and you will not be judged. Do not condemn, and you will not be condemned. Forgive, and you will be forgiven. Give, and it will be given to you"* (Luke 6:37-38).

God has planted a specific seed toward every harvest He desires. When God wants a love harvest, He plants love. When God wants good people, He plants seeds of His goodness on earth. When God wanted sons and daughters, He planted His Son.

**10. The field you sow in will be the field you grow in.**

The anointing you sow into will be the anointing you reap. If you want a specific anointing in your life, sow into the ministry of someone who walks in that anointing. I had a desire to be used by God in the healing ministry, so I began systematically sowing seed into the greatest healing ministries on earth. I needed wisdom, so I sowed seed into a ministry which focuses on wisdom. I was struggling in my Greek New Testament class in college, so I deliberately gave to the ministry of a man who is a brilliant Greek teacher. I wanted to be a crusade evangelist, so I targeted my seed towards crusade evangelists. Each of these seeds produced a harvest in my life.

If you want to eat steak, do not give your money to the hamburger restaurant. Give to those who feed you. If you want your real estate holdings to grow, do not invest in the stock market. If you want some new clothes, give away some of the new clothes in your closet. Do not give away your old, ugly clothes or you will receive a harvest in worn out clothing. If you give junk away, you will receive a one hundred-fold return on junk you do not like. Give your best away and God will multiply the same back into your life. Do you want to get out of debt? Give to your church to help them get out of debt. Your harvest will come where you focus your seed.

**11. The earth is required to bring forth a harvest.**

God commanded the earth to produce harvests (Genesis 1:24). This command has never been rescinded. The only time the ground

**Everything you need is hidden in a seed.**

Where is an apple tree? In a seed.
Where is a corn cob? In a seed.
Where is your dream house? In a seed.
Where is your new car? In a seed.

does not have to produce a harvest is when no seed is planted. But every time a seed enters the ground, the dirt is required to produce a harvest.

**12. Seeds are God's plan for man's provision.**

God told Adam and Eve, *"I give you every seed-bearing plant on the face of the whole earth and every tree that has fruit with seed in it. They will be yours for food"* (Genesis 1:29). Sowing and reaping is the only legitimate source for God's provision.

**13. Both God and man are involved in making harvest time come.**

*"...No plant of the field had yet sprung up, for the LORD God had not sent rain on the earth and there was no man to work the ground"* (Genesis 2:5) According to this verse, there are two elements for every harvest.

1. God does His part by sending rain.
2. You do your part by working the ground.

This means that until you get out in the fields and sow some seed, you will never receive a harvest. Until you sow seed, God has nothing to work with when trying to bless you. You need to put some seed in the ground before you pray for a harvest. A lot of Christians are wondering why God is not answering their prayer requests; meanwhile God is wondering why they are not sowing any seed. God cannot send a harvest where there has been no seed planted.

**14. Once God set the laws of seedtime and harvest in motion, even He obeys those laws.**

*"...the LORD God planted a garden eastward in Eden; and there He put the man whom He had formed"* (Genesis 2:8 - KJV). Notice that God planted the garden. When God wanted to create a special place for Adam and Eve, He could have spoken a word and the garden would have appeared from thin air, but instead God chose to follow His own rules. Instead of creating a garden, God planted a garden. If God used the laws of seedtime to create, then shouldn't we use those same laws?

**15. God wants you to be rich.**

The first directions in the Bible are a treasure map leading directly to gold. First, God placed Adam and Eve in a beautiful garden, then He gave them geographic instructions on how to find the purest gold. *"The name of the first [river] is the Pishon; it winds through the entire land of Havilah, where there is gold. (The gold of that land is good; pearls and onyx are also there)"* (Genesis 2:11-12). If God did not want mankind to be rich, why would He tell the first man and woman how to find gold?

**16. Satan is a taker.**

We already learned that God is a Giver, equally important to understand is that Satan is a taker. Satan was the serpent who deceived Eve into disobeying God. Jesus said, *"The thief comes only to steal and kill and destroy"* (John 10:10). Satan introduced sin and death into the world, he stole man's fellowship with God, and he destroyed God's perfect creation.

**17. Partaking of a forbidden harvest is sin.**

*"...the LORD God commanded the man, 'You are free to eat from any tree in the garden; but you must not eat from the tree of the knowledge of good and evil, for when you eat of it you will surely die'"* (Genesis 2:16-17). Satan tempted Eve by offering a harvest she had no right to eat. She sinned by eating the fruit of forbidden seed.

Satan often tempts people by offering them a harvest they have not earned through sowing. I recently read of a pastor in Africa

## God's Nature is Revealed by the Seed

The principles of sowing and reaping are an integral part of God's nature. Thus it should come as no surprise to see these principles at work in several different realms of His creation.

The Realm of Nature

A farmer sows seed in the ground, roots go down, and a shoot grows upward. When the plant matures, it produces a harvest of many seeds.

The Realm of Reproduction

A man sows a seed into a woman. A baby grows and is born nine months later. The Bible refers to the child as the seed of his or her parents. For example, the Jews (and Christians by adoption) are called the "seed of Abraham."

The Realm of the Spiritual

A believer sows seed (money, time, resources) into the kingdom of God. God rewards the faithfulness with a harvest of blessings.

Each of these realms of seed-sowing reveal principles which are applicable to the other realms. All truth is parallel. The higher truth of God's nature is reflected throughout His creation.

who started a car theft ring so he would appear prosperous to his congregation. If a harvest involves dishonesty, exploitation, unethical behavior, or theft, it is a false harvest and partaking of that harvest is sin.

**18. The curse of sin is a corruption of the seed-growing process.**

Eve's curse was difficulty in seed-bearing. Originally, Eve would have had an easy time during birth, but sin caused the birthing process to be painful. *"To the woman [God] said, 'I will greatly increase your pains in childbearing; with pain you will give birth to children...'"*(Genesis 3:16).

Adam's curse was difficulty in seed-growing. Originally, Adam did not have to work hard to find food because all the trees and plants yielded their fruit to his hands. But, after he sinned, growing food became difficult. God said to Adam, *"Cursed is the ground because of you; through painful toil you will eat of it all the days of your life. It will produce thorns and thistles for you, and you will eat the plants of the field. By the sweat of your brow you will eat your food..."* (Genesis 3:17-19).

* Sin birthed evil seeds like thorns and thistles to compete with good seeds.

* Sin brought a curse on the ground, making it difficult for good seeds to bear fruit.

* Sin turned farming into a sentence of hard labor for Adam and his descendants.

Man was meant to be above the seed-growing process but since death involves returning to dust, man became part of the seed-growing process. He literally became soil for seeds to grow in. *"By the sweat of your brow you will eat your food until you return to the ground, since from it you were taken; for dust you are and to dust you will return"* (Genesis 3:19).

**19. God's answer to His biggest problem was seed.**

God told the serpent, *"I will put enmity between thee and the woman, and between thy seed and her seed; it shall bruise thy head, and thou shalt bruise his heel"* (Genesis 3:15- KJV). It was the Seed of the woman (Jesus) who was destined to crush the devil's head. Our answer to our biggest problem is seed!

**20. Bad seed always grows weeds.**

Sin has consequences. The moment Adam and Eve sinned, they planted a bad seed which became a time bomb which would repeatedly explode in their future. The seed of death entered the world but did not produce fruit until the day that Cain killed Abel. What can we learn from the children of Adam and Eve?

## How the Power of the Seed Revolutionized my Life

I was on my way to the home of Oral and Evelyn Roberts when God taught me a lesson about seed-sowing. God whispered a command to me, "Daniel, I want you to give to My servant." He reminded me that the concept of seedtime and harvest had originally been revealed to Dr. Roberts.

Suddenly, I felt so foolish. I had been about to enter the presence of the man of God without being ready to sow a seed into his life. God saved me from what could have been the worst mistake of my life.

I asked God how much I should give. He said, "Give Oral Roberts $1,000." When I heard God's answer, I almost went into shock. Let me explain.

When we were teenagers, my brother Stephen and I traveled and did children's ministry for churches all over America. I can tell you from experience, no one gets rich off the offerings in children's church. One time we received an offering of $5.73. I was so excited I went and bought a can of silly string to use at our next show. Another time we received the abundant blessing of $13.53. Some churches would give us $50, other churches would give us $100. After traveling thousands of miles to dozens of churches, we had managed to save and scrape together $1,000. We had big plans for that money. We were going to use it to go on a mission trip.

Now God was asking me to give away my hard-earned money. I wanted to make sure I was hearing the voice of God so I leaned over to my brother and explained I wanted to plant a seed. I asked him to pray about how much we should give. He prayed and God spoke the same number to him He had spoken to me.

As we made out the check, God spoke to me again. He promised, "If you obey Me and give the $1,000, I will bless your ministry." Then God continued with a question, "Do you want Me to bless your personal finances as well?" I realized God was giving me an opportunity to sow even more seed in exchange for an even greater harvest.

The first time God spoke to me to give, it was a command. The second time God spoke, it was an invitation to experiment with the power of the seed. I did not have much in my personal bank account but I made out another check for $100. Later as we placed the $1,100 in the hands of Oral Roberts, I felt a tremendous anointing enter the room. Giving never felt so liberating.

I can honestly tell you that since that time, God has blessed me more than I could have imagined. Our ministry went from receiving checks for a hundred dollars to receiving checks for thousands of dollars. God gave me the idea for a book and that idea has brought thousands of dollars into the ministry. My personal finances have been abundantly blessed. I graduated from Oral Roberts University completely debt-free (my parents did not have to pay anything). Even more exciting, the healing anointing has come upon my life and when I preach, people get healed by Jesus. All this can be traced back to my $1,100 seed.

Understand this, Oral Roberts did not need my money. In his lifetime he raised over 1.5 billion dollars for the kingdom of God. My $1,100 was not going to impress him. God did not tell me to give because Dr. Roberts needed the money; God told me to give because I needed the harvest.

That $1,100 was the best money I have ever invested. It destroyed the spirit of poverty in my life.

Mike Murdock talks about how a $1,000 seed he planted "broke the back of poverty" in his life. Recently, I jokingly asked God why Dr. Murdock got to give $1,000 and I had to give $1,100 to destroy poverty. God joked right back and replied, "Inflation."

**The body of Christ has enough to meet every need if everyone does his or her part.**

Once, a pastor stood before his church and announced, "I've got some good news and some bad news. The good news is that the church has all the money it needs...the bad news is that it is all still in your wallets."

**Sometimes, the body of Christ is not as generous as it could be.**

Once, there were two old dollar bills. One was a $100 dollar bill and the other was a $1 dollar bill. The $100 dollar bill said, "I've lived a good life. I've been to the amusement park, the theater, the zoo and baseball games." "Wow," said the $1 dollar bill. You sure have had a good life." "Where have you been?" asked the $100 dollar bill. "Oh, I've been to a Baptist church, a Methodist church, a Lutheran church and an Episcopal church." The $100 bill asked, "What's a church?"

# Secrets of the Seed From Cain, Abel, and Seth

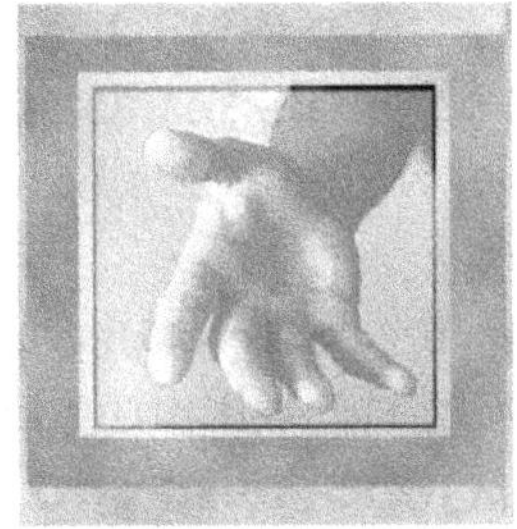

**21. The lesson of Cain: Bad seed will create your greatest tragedy.**

Cain was the first baby ever born. Eve pinned high hopes on him. She probably expected Cain to be the seed that would crush the serpent's head. But alas, it was not to be. Instead of crushing the serpent, he killed his brother. If you plant bad seed, be ready to reap a bad harvest.

**22. The lesson of Abel: Your greatest tragedy will be when your bad seed kills your good seed.**

Both Cain and Abel were the seed of Adam and Eve. Their greatest tragedy came when they discovered the bloody body of their son Abel and realized the full consequences of their mistake in disobeying God. It was sad when they lost the garden, but it was tragic when they lost their son. You may feel like this happens in your life. Since you became a Christian, you have been planting good seeds, but it may seem like you are still reaping a harvest from the bad seeds you scattered during your old lifestyle. But keep reading for the good news.

**23. The lesson of Seth: God's greatest mercy is when He replaces lost seed with new seed.**

The consequences of sin remained. God did not raise Abel from the dead, but God did send another son named Seth. It was this seed of Eve whose descendant would eventually give birth to the Messiah.

God forgives you, but He will not stop the consequences of bad seed. God's law says, "Seedtime and harvest will never cease." Every seed, both good and bad, will produce a harvest in your future. For example, David sowed bad seed when he slept with Uriah's wife; he reaped the consequences when his son Absalom rebelled. God forgave him, but he still had to pay a price for his sin.

Because of your past, you have suffered tragedies and lost opportunities. The scars from those mistakes will always be with you. Those lost opportunities will always be lost. But I have good news for you!

God will replace the seed you have lost with new seed. He will give you another chance. He will provide new opportunities. Adam and Eve made mistakes when raising Cain and Abel, but they did a better job with Seth.

**Five Steps to Receiving a Harvest**

1. Tithing plows your field.
A farmer must hoe before he can sow.
2. Giving sows your seed.
3. Prayer waters your ground.
4. Repentance uproots your weeds.
5. God grows your harvest.

# <u>Secrets of the Seed</u> From the Life of Noah

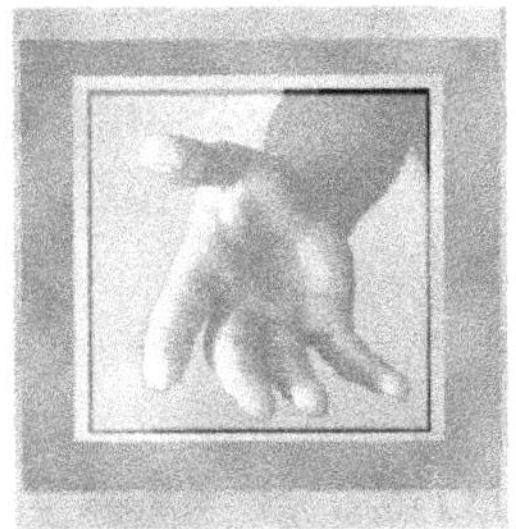

**24. The greatest seed we can sow is obedience.**

God told Noah to build an ark because it was going to rain. No one had ever built an ark before. It had never rained before. As far as Noah was concerned, these were nonsense words. Would you obey if God told you to build a foofal because it is going to nargle?

Noah went to enormous expense and effort to build the ark. His neighbors laughed at him as he built a gigantic boat miles away from the nearest water. They laughed again when he started turning his boat into a zoo. Yet, *"Noah did everything just as God commanded him"* (Genesis 6:22). Noah sowed a seed of obedience and reaped a harvest of survival when everyone else in the world died. What can we learn about obedience from Noah's situation?

**25. Obedience is the difference between survival and extinction.**

If Noah had disobeyed, he would have died in the flood. One preacher tells a story about an instruction from the Holy Spirit not to get on a particular airplane flight. It did not make sense to him until later when he heard the airplane had crashed.

**26. When God gives specific instructions, He expects exact obedience.**

As you read the story of Noah, you discover God gave him precise instructions concerning the material the ark was to be built from, the exact measurements of the ark, how to seal the water out, where to put the door, how many decks were needed on the inside, whom to take on the ark, the number of animals to load, and instructions concerning food. Failure to obey any one of these instructions would have resulted in catastrophe.

**27. Half-way obedience has the same results as disobedience.**

What if Noah had built a smaller boat? What if Noah had failed to cover the ark with pitch? What if Noah had forgotten to load a species of animals? Small disobedience leads to big problems.

**28. Each of God's instructions has a reason, even if that reason is not apparent yet.**

God told Noah to load seven pairs of all the clean animals and one pair of all the other animals. Noah did not discover the reason for this instruction until after the flood when he wanted to sacrifice a burnt offering to the Lord. When the appropriate time came for Noah to offer a sacrifice to the Lord, he remembered that God had already provided for the sacrifice through His instructions. Noah sacrificed some of the extra clean animals.

God will never ask you to sacrifice something He has not already provided for through His previous instructions to you. One time I felt prompted to put some money aside in my savings account. I did not know why until an opportunity came several months later to plant some seed into a significant ministry. If I had not obeyed the prompting, I would have missed out on the chance to bless someone.

When God gives you an instruction, obey it, even if it does not make sense yet. As time passes, the reason behind the instruction will become obvious. God is not specifically interested in having your seed; He has plenty of seed. God does not really need your money, but He craves your obedience to His instructions. The opportunity to sow seed is an opportunity to show your obedience.

**29. Extra seed must be set aside during times of devastation in order to prepare for times of restoration.**

Noah had to take seed on the ark (Genesis 6:21). If he had taken just enough grain to feed his animals, he would not have been able to replant after the flood. In obedience to God, Noah prepared for the day sowing would once again be possible.

**30. Seedtime and harvest will never cease.**

*"As long as the earth endures, seedtime and harvest, cold and heat, summer and winter, day and night will never cease"* (Genesis 8:22). Is the earth still here? Is summer hot and winter cold? Does day still follow night? Then seedtime and harvest is still part of God's pattern of life. It always has been and always will be the way God provides for His people.

**31. Seedtime always precedes harvest.**

*"...seedtime and harvest..."* (Genesis 8:22). Notice that this verse does not say "harvest and seedtime" because the harvest never comes before sowing. Sometimes we think, "After I get a lot of money, then I will give," but that is not how God works. He says give and then you will get. You must sow before you can reap.

**32. The answer to complete devastation is sowing seed.**

The flood interrupted the cycle of sowing and reaping. This interruption was caused by man's wickedness. If you interrupt the process of sowing and reaping in your life, it will cause devastation. The only way to restart the harvests is to restart the sowing.

During Noah's flood, the earth was destroyed. All the plants and animals died in the great deluge. When Noah stepped from the ark, he viewed a wasteland of muddy filth. What was God's solution to the problem? In response to the utter devastation, God reminded Noah of the principles of sowing and reaping. When you suffer loss in your life, sow some seed as quickly as possible so your restoration can begin immediately.

God commanded Noah to continue the cycle of sowing and reaping, *"As for you, be fruitful and increase in number; multiply on the earth and increase upon it"* (Genesis 9:7), and God established a covenant with Noah and with all his seed (Genesis 9:9).

### My $80,000 Harvest

When it was time for me to begin college, my parents informed me they did not have any money to help me pay tuition. Since I desired to go to Oral Roberts University (which had a $20,000 yearly price tag) it looked impossible for me to pay for my education, but I never wavered in my faith in God's provision.

The summer before attending ORU, I wondered where the money for the first semester was going to come from. I knew I should plant a seed, but I was so poor I did not have any money to give away. In the natural, I should have found a job flipping hamburgers in order to be able to save for school, but instead I felt led by God to donate my time to a church. For six months, I gave eight hours of every day as a seed into the kingdom of God, and when the time came for me to start school, God provided for the first semester. If you have no money, use your time as a seed.

Four years later, God had provided for my complete tuition through scholarships, grants, and other surprises. By planting a seed of my time into my home church, I received a harvest worth over $80,000! I graduated from Oral Roberts University completely debt free.

# Secrets of the Seed From the Life of Abraham

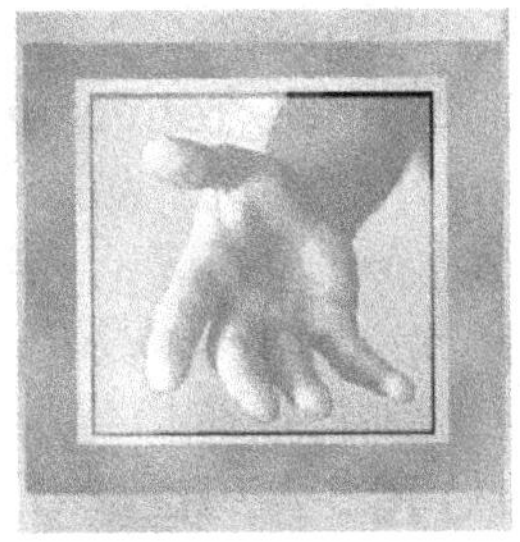

**33. We are blessed so we can be a blessing.**

God promised Abraham, *"... I will bless you...and you will be a blessing"* (Genesis 12:2). We receive harvests so we can be a harvest in the life of someone in need.

**34. Be careful which fields you plant in.**

Lot, the nephew of Abraham, discovered that a field of greener grass is not always the best choice. Abraham and Lot decided to separate, and as a generous gesture, Abraham gave Lot the choice of where he wanted to live. *"Lot looked up and saw that the whole plain of the Jordan was well watered...So Lot chose for himself the whole plain of the Jordan and set out toward the east. The two men parted company: Abram lived in the land of Canaan, while Lot lived among the cities of the plain and pitched his tents near Sodom. Now* ***the men of Sodom were wicked and were sinning greatly against the LORD****"* (Genesis 13:10-13). Lot made a good choice from a natural standpoint, but the area he chose to live in was saturated with sin.

A few chapters later (Genesis 19), we find Lot living inside Sodom at the same time God decided to destroy Sodom and Gomorrah. Lot ends up losing virtually everything he owns, including his wife. A green field full of sin is guaranteed to produce a negative harvest.

**35. Paying the tithe predates the law of Moses.**

In Genesis 14, four kings attacked an alliance of five kings and defeated them. One of their captives was Lot, the nephew of Abraham. When news of this reached Abraham, he called out an army of 318 trained men born in his household and went in pursuit. During the night he divided his men to attack and he defeated them. He recovered all the goods that had been stolen and brought back his relative Lot and all the other captives.

After Abraham returned from winning the battle, *"the king of Sodom came out to meet him in the...King's Valley. Then Melchizedek king of Salem brought out bread and wine. He was priest of God Most High, and he blessed Abram, saying, 'Blessed be Abram by God Most High, Creator of heaven and earth....' Then* ***Abram gave him a tenth of everything"*** (Genesis 14:17-20).

Notice that Melchizedek was the priest of God Almighty and he blessed Abraham. He functioned as Abraham's spiritual leader and in response Abraham gave him a tenth (a tithe) of all the spoils he won in battle. We find out more about this mysterious priest in Hebrews 7:1-5 *"This Melchizedek was king of Salem and priest of God Most High. He met Abraham returning from the defeat of the kings and blessed him, and Abraham gave him a tenth of everything. First, his name means 'king of righteousness;' then also, 'king of Salem' means 'king of peace.' Without father or mother, without genealogy, without beginning of days or end of life, like the Son of God he remains a priest forever. Just think how great he was: Even the patriarch Abraham gave him a tenth of the plunder!"*

Some think modern believers do not need to tithe because tithing is part of the law of Moses and we have been set free from the law. However, as we can see from this story, the practice of tithing predates the law of Moses. The writer of Hebrews points out that even Levi, the priest to whom the Israelites tithed, also tithed through his ancestor Abraham (Hebrews 7:5-10).

**36. Seed-sowers look to God as their Source, not to man.**

After Abraham rescued his nephew Lot (and inadvertently rescued the five kings) the king of Sodom offered to make Abraham a rich man, but Abraham refused to accept anything from the king because he wanted everyone to know that God was his Source, not man. When the king of Sodom offered to give Abraham all the spoils of the victory, Abraham said, *"I will accept nothing belonging to you, not even a thread or the thong of a sandal, so that you will never be able to say, 'I made Abraham rich.' I will accept nothing..."* (Genesis 14:21-24).

Abraham was forced to look to God as his Source because it was impossible for any man to supply what he really wanted. Abraham was already wealthy beyond belief. His only problem was his lack of an heir. He did not need a harvest of money; he already had money. He needed the harvest of a son. *"After* [tithing to the priest Melchizedek], *the word of the LORD came to Abram in a vision: 'Do not be afraid, Abram. I am your shield, your very great reward.' But Abram said, 'O Sovereign LORD, what can You give me since I remain childless and the one who will inherit my estate is Eliezer of Damascus?' And Abram said, 'You have given me no children; so a servant in my household will be my heir.' Then the word of the LORD came to him: 'This man will not be your heir, but a son coming from your own body will be your heir.' He took him outside and said, 'Look up at the heavens and count the stars, if indeed you can count them.' Then He said to Him, 'So shall your offspring be.' Abram believed the LORD, and He credited it to him as righteousness"* (Genesis 15:1-6).

In the King James Bible, the word used for "children" and "offspring" is the word "seed." This reflects the fact that the original Hebrew actually uses the word "seed" to refer to children. Children are the seed of their parents. In response to Abraham's act of tithing to Melchizedek, God promised to give him a seed (Isaac), plus God promised to give him more children than the number of stars that are in the sky. Now that is a harvest!

**37. Do not plant where God has not told you to plant.**

Abraham's greatest tragedy was when he impregnated Hagar instead of waiting for God to work a miracle in the body of his wife

Sarah (Genesis 16). Essentially, he planted his seed in the wrong womb. Instead of waiting for his harvest from a God-ordained field, he scattered seed in the wrong field. Hagar bore a son she named Ishmael. He became the father of the Islamic nations, and we are still reaping the negative effects of this harvest in modern times.

**38. God blesses you in order to fulfill His covenant with Abraham.**

Part of the covenant promise is the activation of the principles of multiplication and fruitfulness. The LORD appeared to Abraham and said, *"...I will confirm My covenant between Me and you and will greatly increase your numbers....this is My covenant with you...I will make you very fruitful....I will establish My covenant as an everlasting covenant between Me and you and your descendants after you..."* (Genesis 17:1-7). God wants to bless you with supernatural riches because He is obligated to fulfill His covenant with Abraham.

The blessings of Abraham come to Gentiles through Jesus Christ (Galatians 3:14). *"...Now that you belong to Christ, you are the true children of Abraham. You are his heirs, and now all the promises God gave to him belong to you"* (Galatians 3:29 NLT).

**39. Today's harvest is tomorrow's seed. Yesterday's harvest is today's seed.**

The harvest for Abraham's obedience was a son, Isaac. Later, God asked Abraham to give up Isaac in exchange for a greater harvest. By giving his son to God, Abraham planted the greatest seed a man has ever planted (Genesis 22:1-19).

"Why?" Abraham asked himself as he paused for a moment to look for a mountaintop in the distance. Three nights before, God had spoken to him.

"Abraham," God had said.

Excited to hear the voice of the living God, Abraham replied, "Here I am."

Then Abraham's heart broke as he listened to God's instructions, "Take your son, your only son, Isaac, whom you love, and go to the region of Moriah. Sacrifice him there as a burnt offering on one of the mountains I will tell you about."

That night Abraham tossed and turned as he tried to figure out why God was asking him to sacrifice his only son. This God Jehovah required so much. He remembered the first time the Lord had spoken to him back when he was a young man in the city of Ur. God had commanded him, "Leave your country, your people and your father's household and go to the land I will show you." God also promised, "I will make you into a great nation and I will bless you; I will make your name great, and you will be a blessing…"

For years, Abraham along with his household, had wandered around the land of Canaan in obedience to God's instruction. God had blessed him beyond measure. He had more sheep than could be counted. He was wealthy in gold, camels, and cattle. He had hundreds of servants and was wealthy enough to support his own private army. But Jehovah was not asking for any of his wealth, He was asking for his precious son.

"My God," Abraham whispered, "why do You want my son? Remember how You promised I would be the father of many nations? Do You recall Your guarantee that my descendants will be as innumerable as the grains of sand on the seashore and as many as the stars on a clear night? How can I have any descendants if I kill my son?"

The silence was deafening. God had already spoken. "Lord," Abraham continued, "Do you remember how Isaac was born? I was one hundred years old and my wife was ninety. It was perhaps your greatest miracle to make Sarah's dead womb bear a child. You promised to bless my son Isaac and to establish your covenant with him. How can Your promises be fulfilled if my son is dead?"

All night Abraham continued to wrestle with God's command. He had walked with God for many years and he had never been disappointed. He remembered that Isaac was a gift from God. Finally, he decided to trust Jehovah even though it did not seem to make sense.

Early the next morning, Abraham got up and prepared his donkey for the journey. He called two of his servants and his son Isaac. As they left, they stopped at a small grove of trees and cut enough wood for a burnt offering.

"Why?" Abraham asked himself again. After three days of traveling, his muscles were sore. In the distance, he saw the place where God wanted him to sacrifice his son.

He said to his servants, "Stay here with the donkey while I

and the boy go over there. We will worship and then we will come back to you." Abraham paused and wondered how they would both return since he was fully intending to kill his son. "Perhaps God will raise him from the dead."

Abraham took the wood off the back of the donkey and asked Isaac to help carry it. He picked up a knife and a small oil lamp. "I will carry these so my son will not cut or burn himself," Abraham thought, then smiled as he realized how ironic the thought was.

The two of them began climbing. Isaac spoke up and said to his father, "Daddy?"

"Yes, my son?" Abraham replied.

"The fire and wood are here," Isaac said, "but where is the lamb for the burnt offering?"

Abraham answered, "God Himself will provide the lamb for the burnt offering, my son."

When they reached the place God had told him about, Abraham built an altar there and arranged the wood on it. With tears in his eyes, he bound his son Isaac and laid him on the altar, on top of the wood. Then he reached out his hand and took the knife to slay his son.

He raised the knife high above his head and was about to plunge it into the breast of Isaac when suddenly he heard a Voice shout, "Abraham! Abraham!"

"Here I am," he replied.

"Do not lay a hand on the boy," the Voice said. "Do not do anything to him. Now I know that you fear God, because you have not withheld from Me your son, your only son." Abraham realized his question had been answered; God had been testing him.

With relief Abraham lowered the knife and looked up. Right in front of him was a ram caught by its horns in a thicket of thorns. He went over and took the ram and sacrificed it as a burnt offering instead of his son.

As Abraham and Isaac walked down together they named the mountain "Jehovah Jireh" which means, "The LORD will provide."

**40. God tests us by asking us to give away that which we care for the most.**

God tested Abraham by asking him to sacrifice his most precious possession. Abraham loved Isaac. For years Abraham patiently waited for this son to be born. When the baby finally arrived, this patriarch rejoiced because Isaac represented the beginning of the fulfillment of all of God's promises to make him a father of many nations. So, Isaac was more than just a son, he represented Abraham's destiny. God was asking Abraham to plant an exceptional seed.

God may test you by asking you to give up that which you consider most valuable. It is easy to say God is number one in your life, but how will you know it is true until you plant an exceptional seed?

**41. God is Jehovah Jireh, the God who provides.**

This story is the first time in the Bible where God reveals Himself as Jehovah Jireh, the God who provides. Abraham's obedience released an aspect of God's character that had never been seen before. As Abraham and Isaac were walking up one side of the mountain, the ram was being led up the other side of the mountain by an angel. God's provision appeared in response to the faith of Abraham. What kind of God are you serving? John Avanzini asks, "Are you serving Jehovah Jireh, or Jehovah-Needy?" Jesse Duplantis asks, "Is your God El-Shaddai or El-Cheapo?" When your need is the greatest, know that God has already provided.

**42. Obedience releases God's blessing.**

Abraham's willingness to sacrifice his son was a seed which produced a wonderful harvest. Abraham's sacrifice opened the door for God to sacrifice His Son, Jesus Christ. Scholars tell us that Mount Moriah was the place which was later called Mount Calvary where Jesus hung on the cross. Because Abraham was willing to give his son, God was able to give His Son.

**43. A moment of giving can release a lifetime of receiving.**

Abraham sent his servant to the city of Nahor in order to find his son a wife. The servant prayed, *"O LORD, God of my master*

*Abraham, give me success today, and show kindness to my master Abraham. See, I am standing beside this spring, and the daughters of the townspeople are coming out to draw water. May it be that when I say to a girl, 'Please let down your jar that I may have a drink,' and she says, 'Drink, and I'll water your camels too,' let her be the one You have chosen for Your servant Isaac"* (Genesis 24:12-14). Before he had finished praying, Rebekah came out with her jar on her shoulder. Not only was she beautiful on the outside, she revealed her inward beauty when Abraham's servant asked her for a drink. In addition to giving him a drink, she drew enough to give all ten of his camels a drink (not an easy task when you think about how much water ten thirsty camels can gulp down).

Her reward began immediately. The servant gave her a gold nose ring and two gold bracelets. Then he told her relatives about the riches of Abraham, *"The LORD has blessed my master abundantly, and he has become wealthy. He has given him sheep and cattle, silver and gold, menservants and maidservants, and camels and donkeys. My master's wife Sarah has borne him a son in her old age, and he has given him everything he owns. And my master made me swear an oath, and said, '...go to my father's family and to my own clan, and get a wife for my son'"* (Genesis 24:35-38). The servant asked Rebekah if she would marry Isaac. When she said "yes" he began showering her with presents of gold and silver jewelry and articles of clothing.

Because of Rebekah's one act of kindness to a traveling stranger, she became the wife of one of the richest men of her day. You never know which deed, planted as a seed, will produce your greatest harvest. Remember the teaching of Jesus, if you give a drink to a thirsty man you have really given a drink to Jesus (Matthew 25:37-40). A seed as simple as a cup of cold water can produce a lifetime of harvest.

# Secrets of the Seed From the Life of Isaac

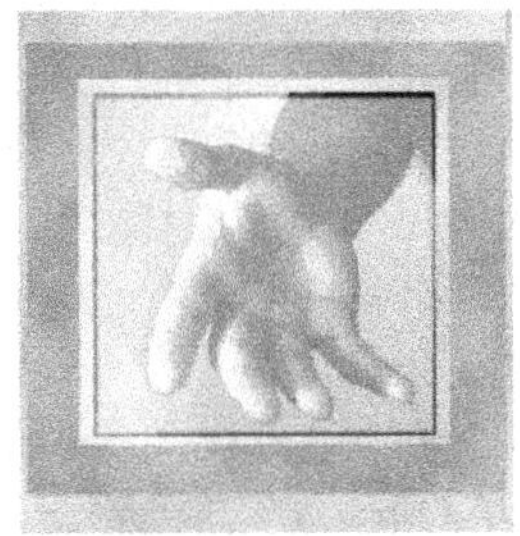

**44. Seeds continue to produce harvests long after those who planted them are dead.**

Isaac was blessed because of his father Abraham. Right now you are reaping a harvest from the seeds past generations of Christians have planted. One of the reasons America has been blessed is because of the seeds planted by our founding fathers.

My grandparents were missionaries in Afghanistan, my parents were missionaries in Mexico, now I am reaping harvests of souls from seeds they planted. The greatest harvest of the seeds you plant today will be reaped by your children and your children's children (should the Lord tarry). Your seed guarantees the harvest of future generations.

One of my great-aunts lived a frugal lifestyle. She ate the plainest food, dressed conservatively, and seldom traveled. She saved every penny of her income and invested it. We thought she was poor but to my family's surprise, when she died she left a fortune of more than a million dollars. Her will stipulated the money be given to a variety of ministries. One university received a hundred thousand dollars, another evangelistic ministry was given a quarter million dollars, a third ministry received another quarter million. At first my family was disappointed she had not given us the money. But later we began to thank God for all the seed she had sown. Since she is in heaven, she is partaking of a wonderful harvest, but here on earth my family asked God for a generational harvest off the seed she sowed. Sure enough, the university she gave money to was happy to give scholarships to several members of my family. Her seed produced a generational harvest for my family.

**45. The 100-fold return can be yours...this year!**

The hundredfold return is mentioned five times in the Bible. The parable of the sower (Matthew 13, Mark 4, Luke 8) reveals that the Word of God can potentially bring a hundredfold return. In Mark 10:29-30, the hundredfold return is promised to those who give up something for the sake of Jesus or for the sake of the gospel.

In order to understand the hundredfold return, we must first look at the story of Isaac. *"Now **there was a famine in the land**, besides the earlier famine of Abraham's time, and Isaac went to Abimelech king of the Philistines in Gerar. The LORD appeared to Isaac and said, 'Do not go down to Egypt; live in the land where I tell you to live. Stay in this land for a while, and I will be with you and will bless you. For to you and your descendants I will give all these lands and will confirm the oath I swore to your father Abraham. I will make your descendants as numerous as the stars in the sky and will give them all these lands, and through your seed all nations on earth will be blessed, because Abraham obeyed Me and kept My requirements, My commands, My decrees and My laws.' So Isaac stayed in Gerar...**Isaac planted crops in that land and the same year reaped a hundredfold, because the LORD blessed him**"* (Genesis 26:1-6, 12).

**46. Plant, even in the midst of difficult economic times.**

There was famine in the land. They were experiencing bad economic times. The ground was hard, the wells had dried up, there was no hope for rain. Yet even in the midst of famine, Isaac still planted crops.

**47. Plant in the land God tells you to live in.**

God specifically told Isaac not to go to Egypt. If Isaac had gone to Egypt, he never would have received the hundredfold return. This principle is important for today's Christians. Many believers jump from church to church looking for the "blessing of the month." But I believe your best harvest will come when you remain faithful in the church God tells you to be in. You will never receive the hundredfold return if you are jumping from field to field scattering seed all over the place.

Why did Isaac think about going to Egypt? His father had gone to Egypt in the midst of a previous famine (Genesis 12:10) and God had blessed him there. But God's plan for blessing Isaac was different from His plan for blessing Abraham. Just because someone did something in a particular way in the past does not mean God wants you to do the same thing. The way God plans to bless you may be different from the way He has blessed others. Listen closely to God and find His plan for your life.

**48. Hear God's promise and act on it.**

God promised Isaac he would be blessed and Isaac acted on this promise by sowing seed. It is important for us to put action behind our faith. God's promises are always conditional: if we do not take action, we will not be blessed.

**49. Believe for the hundredfold return on your seed in the SAME YEAR you plant it.**

*"Isaac planted crops in that land and the same year reaped a hundredfold..."* (Genesis 26:12). Some people plant seed and expect to reap years later, but I think we should believe for harvest to come the same year that we plant seed. If you will believe for it, you will begin to see it happening. The reason Isaac received the hundredfold return was "*...because the LORD blessed him*" (Genesis 26:12).

**50. With the Lord's blessing, you can go from rich...to very wealthy!**

Isaac *"became rich, and his wealth continued to grow until he became very wealthy"* (Genesis 26:13). What is "very wealthy?"

I do not fully know, but it is better than just being rich.

* Rich people buy a house...very wealthy people buy estates.

* Rich people fly first-class...very wealthy people fly their own planes.

* Rich people donate to the church building fund...very wealthy people build churches.

Do you want to be rich? Or do you want to be very wealthy? According to your faith be it done unto you.

**51. When God blesses you, some people will be jealous.**

Isaac had *"so many flocks and herds and servants that the Philistines envied him"* (Genesis 26:14).

**52. Satan will do anything he can to stop your crops from growing.**

*"So all the wells that his father's servants had dug in the time of his father Abraham, the Philistines stopped up, filling them with earth"* (Genesis 26:15). Why would anyone fill in a water well? They wanted to stop Isaac's harvest.

Satan is going to play the same trick on you. He will try to dry up your source of income. It will feel like someone is throwing trash into your purified drinking water. But if you hold onto God's promise, *"No weapon that is formed against you shall prosper"* (Isaiah 54:17 -NKJV).

**53. Re-dig the wells the enemy has stopped up.**

Wells are important because crops need water. When enemies try to stop your harvest by putting dirt in your water source, re-dig the wells. *"Isaac reopened the wells that had been dug in the time of his father Abraham, which the Philistines had stopped up after Abraham died....Isaac's servants dug in the valley and discovered a well of fresh water there. But the herdsmen of Gerar quarreled with Isaac's herdsmen and said, 'The water is ours!'...Then they dug another well, but they quarreled over that one also....He moved on from there and dug another well, and no one quarreled over it"* (Genesis 26:18-22).

Isaac was so blessed that no matter where he dug, he struck water. This was a miracle because much of the land of Israel is parched and dry. Isaac's enemies kept stealing his wells, but God kept supplying new ones until the enemies gave up.

God will do the same for you. No matter how many times the enemy comes and steals what belongs to you, God will restore it to you. Eventually the enemy will figure out that it is not worth the bother to steal from you.

**A single seed contains more potential wealth than all the diamond mines of South Africa.**

Once an old farmer was talking to his son. He extended his wrinkled hands out in front of him. Clutched in each fist was an object. "Son," he said, "I am close to dying, but before I go I want to give you an inheritance. You must make a choice between the objects I hold in my two hands."

Slowly he opened his left hand and the young man gasped as he saw a beautiful diamond as big as an acorn. Light sparkled and reflected off the many facets. The luster, clarity, and cut made the diamond an object of breathtaking beauty.

Then the farmer opened his right hand. At first the young man thought it was empty, but then he saw a tiny seed resting on the weathered palm. The seed's dirty roundness inspired no awe.

"Which is more valuable?" asked the old man.

"Obviously, the diamond is worth far more than the seed," replied the son.

"You are wrong."

"I don't understand."

"Let me explain. If I give you this diamond, you could ask a jeweler to cut it up into four pieces and give your wife a beautiful necklace, ring, and earring set. Or, you could sell the diamond for a large sum of money and your whole family could live comfortably off the money for a year. But, this diamond will never grow. It will never be more than what it is right now.

You can divide the diamond or subtract from the diamond, but the diamond will never increase."

The old man began to speak again, "I have been a farmer my whole life. I have witnessed the power of a seed. This small seed may not be much to look at but if you plant it, it will grow and produce a harvest. If you replant your harvest, your original seed will have multiplied many fold. As you continue to sow and reap, this seed will become much more than what it is right now. Contained in this seed is the power to feed a nation for generations to come. Seeds are the greatest commodity in the universe."

Thoughtfully, the young man considered his father's words. Slowly, he reached out his hand and touched the fist containing the seed. "I choose the seed," he said.

With tears of joy welling up in his eyes, the old farmer hugged his son. "Tomorrow I will begin teaching you the principles which have made me rich. I will teach you about sowing and reaping."

now. Contained in this seed is the power to feed a nation for generations to come. Seeds are the greatest commodity in the universe."

Thoughtfully, the young man considered his father's words. Slowly, he reached out his hand and touched the fist containing the seed. "I choose the seed," he said.

With tears of joy welling up in his eyes, the old farmer hugged his son. "Tomorrow I will begin teaching you the principles which have made me rich. I will teach you about sowing and reaping."

# Secrets of the Seed From the Life of Jacob

**54. Even if you have a bad boss and poor wages, God can still bless you.**

For twenty years Jacob worked for his father-in-law, Laban. Ten times Laban cheated him by changing his wages (Genesis 31:41). But God blessed Jacob no matter what Laban did to him. You always reap what you sow, even if you have sown bad seeds. Jacob cheated his brother Esau out of the birthright and the blessing of their father, Isaac (Genesis 27). Jacob deserved to be cheated by Laban. He was reaping a harvest from seeds he had sown. Yet the blessing of God overcame the effects of bad seeds.

When Laban told Jacob he could have all the ugly sheep as his wages, every sheep that was born was ugly. Jacob arrived at Laban's house as a penniless wanderer, and he left as a wealthy man. Why? Because God blessed him in spite of the bad seeds he had sown, his bad boss and his poor wages.

Do not look to your employer as your source or to your paycheck as your harvest. Your blessing is in the hands of God, not in the hands of an earthly boss. Even if your boss cheats you, know that your promotion is in God's hands.

**55. Sowing seed is the only way to erase your past mistakes.**

When Jacob returned to his homeland, he was scared his brother Esau would still be angry with him for having stolen his birthright. Jacob decided to sow a seed into his brother's life. He sent several flocks of animals ahead as a gift for his brother (Genesis 32:13-16).

Esau came with an army of four hundred men, ready to punish Jacob for his deception twenty years before. But on the way, the servants of Jacob kept giving him herds of animals: goats, sheep, camels, cows, and donkeys. In today's terms, if each of the five hundred and eighty animals was worth $1000, Jacob planted a seed valued at over half a million dollars. By the time Esau met Jacob, he was no longer angry with him. They hugged, they kissed, they wept together. It was hard for Esau to be mad at someone who had just given him half a million dollars worth of wealth.

Robb Thompson says, "Sowing seed is the only way to stop the momentum of your mistakes." The only way to destroy the effects of bad seed you have planted in your lifetime is to sow good seed. If you have wronged someone and you want to restore the relationship, try planting some seed into his or her life.

**The seeds you plant form a foundation for your future life.**

Before a skyscraper can be built, the foundations must go deep into the earth. Before a plant can grow up, roots must go down.

# <u>Secrets of the Seed</u> From the Life of Moses

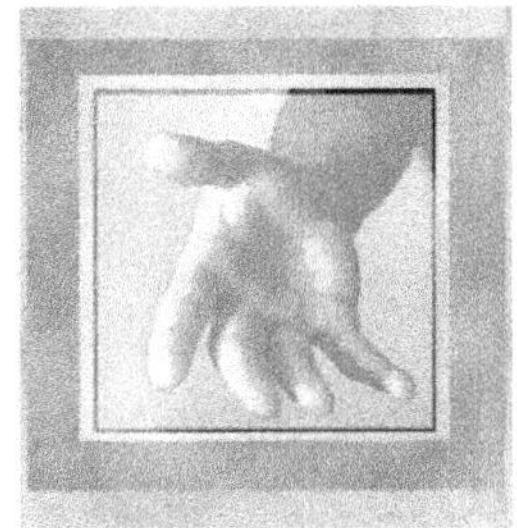

**56. You will always have something in your hand which God can use.**

When Moses was called by God to deliver the Israelites from Egypt, he felt inadequate for the job. He was a poor shepherd living in the desert. He felt like he had nothing to give. But God asked him, *"What is that in your hand?"* (Exodus 4:2).

Moses replied, "A staff."

God said, "Throw it to the ground." He was asking Moses to give up his only possession. In obedience Moses threw it to the ground, and God performed a miracle with the staff.

Later Moses used this staff to deliver Israel from Egypt. Every time he stretched out his staff, a new plague would torment Pharaoh. Moses even used the staff to open up a path through the Red Sea.

Even when it appears like you have nothing, there is something in your hand which is key to your miracle. If you will allow God to use what is in your hand, you will reap a supernatural harvest.

**57. God never wants our second-best.**

Throughout the books of Exodus, Leviticus, and Numbers, God instructs the Israelites concerning the proper sacrifice to put on the altar. Sixty times God specifically tells them to bring an animal *"without blemish."* God did not want inferior animals, only the perfect specimens were worthy of being sacrificed.

The Lord is not interested in being second-place to anything. If you give God your second-best, you are living in idolatry. What is idolatry? It is when you put something else before God in your life. If you give God your second-best, that means that some thing or person is more important to you than your Creator is. Your best becomes an idol the moment you are not willing to give it to God. Does God occupy the number one position in your heart?

**58. Seven Harvests for your life from Exodus 23:20-33.**

1. Protection: *"I am sending an angel ahead of you to guard you..."*
2. Destiny: *"...to bring you to the place I have prepared."*
3. Enemies Destroyed: *"I will be an enemy to your enemies and will oppose those who oppose you...I will wipe them out."*
4. Financial Provision: *"Worship the LORD your God, and His blessing will be on your food and water."*
5. Healing: *"I will take away sickness from among you, and none will miscarry or be barren in your land. I will give you a full life span."*
6. Increase: *"Little by little I will drive them out before you, until you have increased enough to take possession of the land."*
7. Land: *"I will establish your borders..."*

# <u>Secrets of the Seed</u> From the Tabernacle Offering

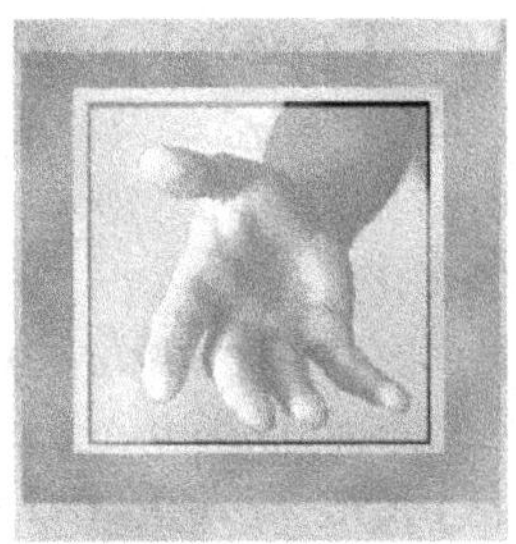

When Moses asked the Israelites to give toward the building of the tabernacle, they responded overwhelmingly. They brought gold, silver, bronze, fine linen, animal skins, spices, and precious stones. The people gave so enthusiastically that Moses was forced to put an end to the offering because they had collected more than enough. Here are some lessons from this great offering.

**59. God asks us to give what we have, not what we do not have.**

Moses said, *"From what you have, take an offering for the LORD..."* (Exodus 35:5). Paul repeats this idea, *"...the gift is acceptable according to what one has, not according to what he does not have"* (2 Corinthians 8:12).

**60. God wants us to be willing to give.**

*"...Everyone who is willing is to bring to the LORD an offering..."* (Exodus 35:5). God never pushes us to give. He leads us. It is the devil who pushes us around. We should never give if we are not

willing to give. This idea is repeated in 2 Corinthians 8:12, *"For if the willingness is there, the gift is acceptable...."*

Coercion, emotional pressure, psychological tricks, and guilt have no place in a proper offering. John Avanzini says, "It is better to give nothing than to give an amount someone pressures you into." If you feel too much pressure to give, wait a few days, and if you still feel God leading you to give, then give.

In the tabernacle offering, only the willing gave. *"All the Israelite men and women who were willing brought to the LORD freewill offerings for all the work the LORD through Moses had commanded them to do"* (Exodus 35:29).

**61. The willingness of God's people to give guarantees abundance in God's house.**

The workers came and told Moses, *'"The people are bringing more than enough for doing the work the LORD commanded to be done.' Then Moses gave an order and they sent this word throughout the camp: 'No man or woman is to make anything else as an offering for the sanctuary.' And so the people were restrained from bringing more, because <u>what they already had was more than enough to do all the work</u>"* (Exodus 36:5-7).

The Israelites were so excited about giving that Moses had to stop the offering. If God's people get willing hearts, then we will see more offerings like this in today's church. Soon after the pastor announces a project, he will be able to tell the people the entire budget has been met. The reason preachers beg and plead for money is because God's people have not been willing givers.

**62. The wealth of the wicked is given to the righteous for the purpose of building God's house.**

Where did all the wealth given in the tabernacle offering come from? The Israelites had been slaves for four hundred years in Egypt. They had been poor, but as they left Egypt, they plundered the entire nation. *"The Israelites did as Moses instructed and asked the Egyptians for articles of silver and gold and for clothing. The LORD had made the Egyptians favorably disposed toward the people, and they gave them what they asked for; so <u>they plundered the Egyptians</u>"* (Exodus 12:35-36).

In one night, they received back wages for four hundred years of labor. As they walked across the Red Sea, the Israelites were the richest homeless people in history. Ironically, God led them out into the wilderness where there were no shops to spend the money. God gave them wealth so the tabernacle could be built.

## Thoughts about Giving

"We make a living by what we earn but we make a life by what we give." - Winston Churchill

"Do not judge today by the harvest you reap but by the seeds you sow." - Robert Louis Stevenson

"The only proof that I am a giver comes on the day I begin to receive." - Robb Thompson

"The seed that leaves your hand never really leaves your life - it simply leaves your hand and goes into your future where it multiplies." - Mike Murdock

"Give according to your income lest God reduces your income according to your giving." - Wayne Myers

"You'll always have everything you want in life if you'll help enough other people get what they want." - Zig Zigler

"A man needs three conversions: first of the heart, then of the head, and lastly, of the purse." - Martin Luther

## Your giving makes you memorable

Two men were shipwrecked on a desert island. Tom immediately began to freak out, "No one knows where we are! We'll never be rescued."

Joe calmly laid down under a palm tree. Tom asked, "How can you be so calm? Don't you know we're going to die on this island?"

Joe explained why he was calm, "I'm very rich."

Tom couldn't believe what he was hearing, "You idiot. Your money means nothing. You can't buy a boat to take you home."

Joe replied, "Yeah, but I'm a tither. My pastor will find me."

# Secrets of the Seed From the Books of the Law

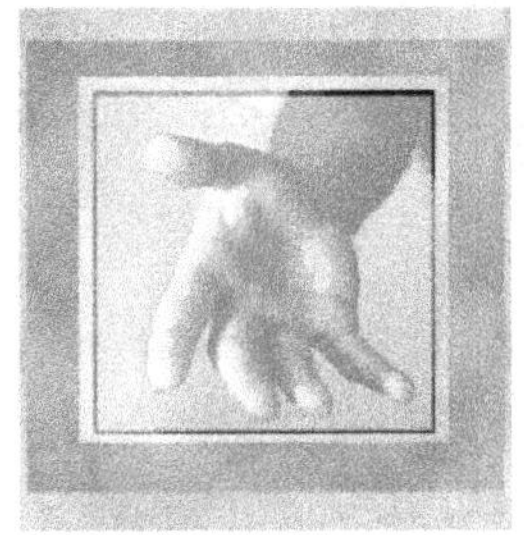

**63. Use part of your harvest to bless the poor.**

*"When you reap the harvest of your land, do not reap to the very edges of your field or gather the gleanings of your harvest. Do not go over your vineyard a second time or pick up the grapes that have fallen. Leave them for the poor and the alien..."* (Leviticus 19:9-10, see also Leviticus 23:22 and Deuteronomy 24:21).

**64. Harvest time can be all the time.**

*"Your threshing will continue until grape harvest and the grape harvest will continue until planting, and you will eat all the food you want..."* (Leviticus 26:5).

**65. God wants you to overflow!**

*"You will still be eating last year's harvest when you will have to move it out to make room for the new"* (Leviticus 26:10).

**66. Son-shine brings harvest and blessing.**

*"The LORD bless you and keep you; the LORD make His face shine upon you and be gracious to you; the LORD turn His face toward you and give you peace"* (Numbers 6:24-26). This was the traditional blessing the priests spoke over the people of Israel.

**67. God wants to give you a land of abundant harvests.**

*"If the LORD is pleased with us, He will lead us into that land, a land flowing with milk and honey, and will give it to us"* (Numbers 14:8).

**68. The thousand-fold return is just the beginning of the blessings God has in store for you.**

*"May the LORD, the God of your fathers, increase you a thousand times and bless you as He has promised!"* (Deuteronomy 1:11).

Recently, I was reading the book of a critic of the seed-faith message. He was whining about the impossibility of receiving a one thousand-fold return. It made me stop and think about the infinite blessings God has in store for His children in heaven. Let us look at some of the costs involved in keeping us in heaven.

The presidential suite at one hotel in New York City is currently available for $22,000 each night, yet it is not nearly as luxurious as your mansion in heaven.

As I write this, gold is selling for $1250 an ounce. At these prices, one mile of heavenly pavement costs God over a billion dollars.

The nicest restaurant in my city costs $90 a plate (before you even order dessert). In heaven you will eat caviar, the best cuts of meat, fresh fruit and vegetables, you will drink two thousand-year-old wine and you do not have to leave a tip. The Lamb's banqueting table is an all-you-can-eat restaurant with style.

Broadway tickets for popular shows sell for $200 or more, yet how can you compare earthly productions to heaven's extravaganza with a cast of 100,000 angels who have been practicing and choreographing for thousands of years? The angels are going to make professional performers look like amateurs.

The thousand-fold return is not only possible, it is the minimum you will receive once you arrive in heaven. You will receive a thousand-fold return on your earthly investment just in your first year in heaven and heaven lasts for eternity! You will receive far more than you can calculate plus as an added bonus you get blessed here in this life as well.

**69. The power to get wealth comes from God.**

*"Remember the LORD your God, for it is He who gives you the ability to produce wealth..."* (Deuteronomy 8:18). The King James Version says God gives us <u>the power</u> to get rich. Every dollar we have ever earned comes from God. Giving back to God is our way of remembering what He has done for us.

Notice that God does not give wealth, instead He gives the "power" to get wealth. This means you cannot just sit around expecting to get rich. You must put your hands to work and put your mind to work and God will give you the ability (creative ideas, diligence, favor, inventions, solutions to problems, etc.) which will make you rich.

**70. God gives the power to get wealth so that His covenant may be established in all the earth.**

It is important not to forget the second half of this verse which tells us what we are supposed to do with our wealth. *"...it is He that giveth thee power to get wealth, <u>that He may establish His covenant...</u>"* (Deuteronomy 8:18 KJV).

**71. Ill-gotten money cannot be used to procure a harvest.**

*"You must not bring the earnings of a female prostitute or of a male prostitute into the house of the LORD your God to pay any vow, because the LORD your God detests them both"* (Deuteronomy 23:18).

## The Blessings of Deuteronomy 28 in Modern Terms

If you fully obey the LORD your God and carefully follow all His commands I give you today (One of the key commands given that day was to be faithful giving your firstfruits and your tithes to God. Read Deuteronomy 26), the LORD your God will set you high above all the nations on earth.

All these blessings will come upon you and follow you wherever you go if you obey the LORD your God:

You will be blessed in the city and blessed in the suburbs.

Your children will be blessed (they will do well in school, in sports, in relationships, and in church). They will be obedient and will grow in wisdom, stature, and in favor with God and man.

The wages of your job will increase, you will receive raises from your boss and year-end bonus checks. The interest rate on your savings account will double, your credit card bills will be paid off. Your real estate will increase in value. Your mortgage will be reduced.

You will get better jobs. Your promotions will come quickly. Your work will be fulfilling and your compensation levels will amaze you. God will bless your diligence and you will have to work less and less for more and more results.

You will have God concepts, insights, and creative ideas for wealth creation and increase. Your strategies will produce abundance for those around you. You will have favor with authorities. You will have prosperous relationships.

Your books will be bestsellers. Your songs will earn royalties. Your movies will receive rave reviews and become blockbusters. Your inventions will be purchased by thousands of people.

Your creative ideas will generate wealth. You will make record breaking sales and your commissions will rise. You will receive estates and inheritances. You will be awarded scholarships and grants.

You will have more than enough to give into the kingdom of God and promote the gospel of Jesus Christ. You will be able to be generous with all those in need. You will support missionaries and give significantly to your church building fund. Your dollars will result in souls being won.

Your spouse will love you all the days of your life and divorce will not darken your marriage nor threaten your financial status.

Your shopping baskets shall overflow. You will find great deals when you are shopping for food. You will find bargain discounts on name-brand clothing. Your cooking will taste great and your food will multiply so you can feed extra people.

You will be blessed when you arrive at work and when you leave for the day.

The LORD will grant that the enemies who rise up against you will be defeated before you. They will come at you from one direction but flee from you in seven. Those who are suing you will drop their cases. Your creditors will forgive your debts. The IRS will rule in your favor. You shall receive warnings but not tickets from policemen.

The LORD will send a blessing on your savings accounts, your checking accounts, your IRAs, and your 401k's. Your investments, your stocks, your bonds, and your mutual funds will multiply in value. Everything you put your hand to (including your hobbies, your jobs, your entrepreneurial ideas) will be blessed. The LORD your God will bless you in the land He is giving you. You will find great deals when purchasing your family home, real estate, rental and commercial properties.

The LORD will establish you as His holy people, as He promised you on oath, if you keep the commands of the LORD your God and walk in His ways.

The LORD will grant you abundant prosperity, in the talents of your children, the increase of your investments and the granting of a lifetime source of income in the land He swore to your forefathers to give you.

You will be healthy all the days of your life.

The LORD will make you the head, not the tail. If you pay attention to the commands of the LORD your God that I give you this day and carefully follow them, you will always be at the top, never at the bottom. You will be a landlord, not a renter; a lender, not a borrower; and a giver, not a taker.

The LORD will open the heavens, the storehouse of His bounty, to send rain on your land in season and to bless all the work of your hands. Then all the peoples on earth will see that you are called by the name of the LORD (Christians), and they will be amazed at your prosperity.

Read the small print...Do not turn aside from any of the commands I give you today, to the right or to the left, following other gods and serving them.

WARNING!, if you do not obey the LORD your God and do not carefully follow all His commands and decrees I am giving you today, be careful because all these blessings will be reversed and you will be cursed. But as long as you keep Jesus the Lord of your life (by obeying His commands) you will be free from the curse!

# Secrets of the Seed From the Life of King Saul

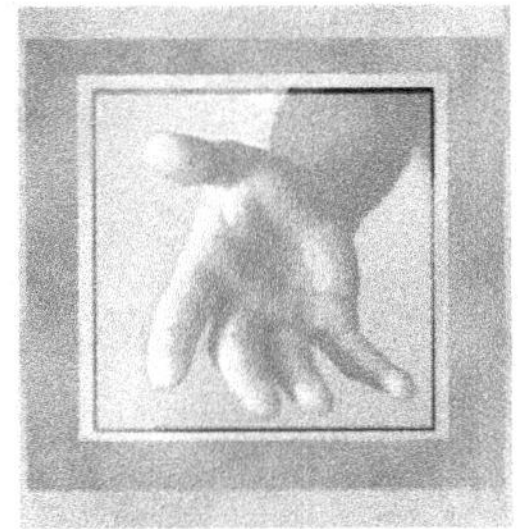

**72. Obedience is better than sacrifice.**

When King Saul went to fight the Amalekites, he was given a divine order to kill all the captured sheep and oxen of the enemy. Instead he kept the best of the animals. When Samuel rebuked him, he tried to excuse his disobedience by explaining that he intended to give those animals as a sacrifice to the Lord. Samuel replied, *"Does the LORD delight in burnt offerings and sacrifices as much as in obeying the voice of the LORD? To obey is better than sacrifice, and to heed is better than the fat of rams"* (1 Samuel 15:22). If you deliberately disobey God and then bring Him an offering, you will find that the Lord will not want your offering. God cannot give a harvest to the disobedient.

## Action Ideas to Increase your Seed-Sowing

- Fast junk food for a week and give the money you save to your church.
- Make a decision not to spend more on clothes than you do on spreading the gospel.
- Instead of taking a family cruise, camp in the mountains for a vacation and give what you save to a missionary.
- Work overtime one night a week and give what you earn to your church.
- Empty the change from your pockets every day into a jar for missions.
- Liquidate some stocks and give the proceeds to God.
- Hold a garage sale and use the money to buy groceries for a poor family.
- Skip going to the movies and give an extra love offering to your pastor.
- When you receive an unexpected harvest, use a predetermined percentage as a seed toward your next harvest.
- Ask God for creative business ideas which will produce wealth for the gospel.
- Invite all your friends over to your house for dinner and introduce them to a missionary. Allow the missionary to talk about his ministry and take up an offering for him.
- Instead of trading in your car to a dealership, give it away.
- Start an investment fund for the purpose of making money for God.

# <u>Secrets of the Seed</u>
# From the Life of King David

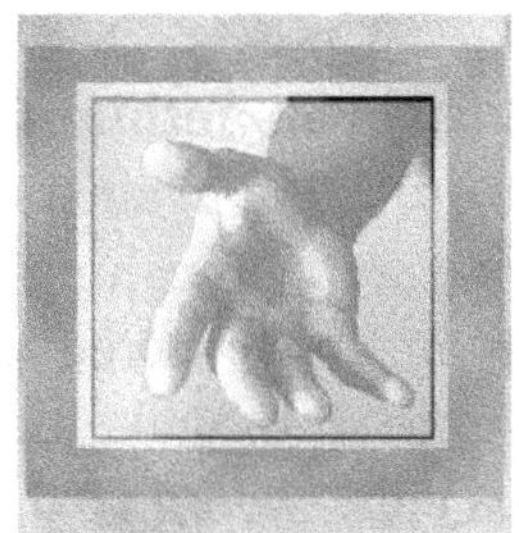

**73. Your giving can promote you from outcast to king.**

When David was a fugitive in the Philistine city of Ziklag, he strategically sent gifts to people all over Israel. (Read 1 Samuel 30:26-31). The people who received these gifts were the ones who later crowned him king.

**74. God is always willing to give you more.**

Nathan the prophet said to David, *"...This is what the LORD, the God of Israel, says: 'I anointed you king over Israel, and I delivered you from the hand of Saul. I gave your master's house to you... I gave you the house of Israel and Judah. And* ***if all this had been too little, I would have given you even more'"***
(2 Samuel 12:7-8).
God gave lavishly to David. God took him:

* from shepherd to king
* from the fields to the palace

* from a fugitive to a ruler
* from poverty to being the richest man in the country
* from anonymity to fame

If all this had been too little, God would have given him even more. We truly serve a lavish God.

**75. Do not let the humbleness of your position reduce the magnitude of your asking.**

David starts his prayer by saying "Who am I?" (2 Samuel 7:18) and finishes his prayer by asking for his house to be blessed forever (2 Samuel 7:29). David says "I am nothing" yet he asks lavishly and God grants his request.

**76. An offering that costs you nothing is worthless.**

When a plague broke out against Israel, the prophet Gad told David to offer a sacrifice at the threshing floor of Araunah. The man who owned the threshing floor offered to give David oxen, wood, and whatever else he needed to make the sacrifice. David refused, explaining, *" 'No, I insist on paying you for it. I will not sacrifice to the LORD my God burnt offerings that cost me nothing." So David bought the threshing floor and the oxen and paid fifty shekels of silver for them"* (2 Samuel 24:24).

**77. A single offering can unleash prosperity for a generation.**

King David wanted to build God a temple, but because he was a man of war, God did not allow him to build the temple. So, David decided to pay for the temple. Robb Thompson asks, "Who is greater? The one who builds a building or the one who pays for it to be built?"

David gathered all the leaders of Israel and gave his entire treasury toward the building of the temple. He said, "With all my resources I have provided for the temple of my God, gold for the gold work, silver for the silver, bronze for the bronze, iron for the iron and wood for the wood, as well as onyx for the settings, turquoise, stones of various colors, and all kinds of fine stone and marble, all of these in large quantities. Besides, in my devotion to the temple of my God I now give my personal treasures of gold and silver for the temple of my God, over and above everything I have provided for this holy temple: three thousand talents (100 tons) of gold and seven thousand talents (260 tons) of refined silver." David's offering would be worth over $1,000,000,000 in today's currency.

Then David asked the leaders of Israel to give. They gave willingly and joyfully. Their offering included over five thousand talents of gold (over 190 tons), ten thousand talents of silver (375 tons), eighteen thousand talents of bronze (675 tons), a hundred thousand talents of iron (3,750 tons), and many precious stones. The value of the people's gift would be worth over $1.5 billion in today's currency.

*"The people rejoiced at the willing response of their leaders, for they had given freely and wholeheartedly to the LORD. David the king also rejoiced greatly"*(1 Chronicles 29:9). Would you rejoice if you were able to take up a $2.5 billion offering?

This one offering ushered in a time of unprecedented wealth in the nation of Israel. God multiplied this amazing seed back into the lives of every leader who gave that day. For a generation, everyone in Israel was wealthy. During Solomon's reign, silver and gold became as common in Jerusalem as stones (2 Chronicles 1:15).

**78. The generous gift of a leader motivates others to give.**

David gave first in the temple offering, then he asked his people to give. Often the giving of a leader sets the pace for the giving of everyone else.

## Every seed has a variety of potentials

What is the potential of an acorn? It can provide food for a squirrel. It could become an oak tree. It could become lumber for a house. It could eventually become a forest. It could be used to make a newspaper which could change the world. A single seed contains the greatest power in the universe.

## Develop a strategy for giving

1. At the beginning of the year prayerfully set a goal for your giving.
2. Make a commitment to tithe to your local church.
3. Give to the places that feed you.
4. Give to those with whom you have relationships.
5. Give up to those who have an anointing you want to flow in.
6. Give down to those who need your anointing.
7. Give to ministries that will produce the greatest harvest for your life.

# Secrets of the Seed From the Life of King Solomon

**79. Our greatest sacrifice releases God's greatest gift.**

*"The king went to Gibeon to offer sacrifices, for that was the most important high place, and Solomon offered a thousand burnt offerings on that altar. At Gibeon the LORD appeared to Solomon during the night in a dream, and God said, 'Ask for whatever you want Me to give you'"* (1 Kings 3:4-5). In one day Solomon offered one thousand burnt offerings. Can you imagine how expensive this must have been? A cow farmer recently told me that a head of cattle sells for about $1,000. In today's prices, Solomon gave God a $1,000,000 sacrifice in one day. In response, God appeared to Solomon and offered him a blank check on a heavenly bank account. God said, "Ask for WHATEVER you want Me to give you."

Solomon could have asked for a long life, for riches, for the death of his enemies, but instead he asked for wisdom. This request pleased God so much that He gave Solomon wisdom, riches, and honor. Solomon became the richest man who ever lived and he was known far and wide for his great wisdom.

**Reasons why your harvest may not have come yet**

Unpaid vows
Failure to tithe
Sowing into bad soil
Inconsistency in giving
Ignoring natural financial laws
Disobedience to the man of God
Failure to recognize your harvest
Failure to obey an instruction from God
Negative words coming from your mouth
Not recognizing the seeds you could plant
Unthankfulness for what God has already done
Looking to man instead of God for your harvest
Failure to target your seed toward a specific need
Trusting in your own abilities instead of trusting in God
Not enough seed in the ground for the size harvest you need

# Secrets of the Seed From the Widow of Zarephath

Famine was devastating the land. In response to Elijah's prophecy to the evil king Ahab, rain ceased falling in Israel. God led Elijah to live by a small stream. Every morning and evening God sent ravens to feed Elijah bread and meat. When the brook dried up, God instructed Elijah to go to a widow in Zarephath. When he arrived, she was gathering sticks outside the gates of the city. He asked her for a drink. As she was going to get it, he also requested a piece of bread.

The widow explained, "As surely as the LORD your God lives, I don't have any bread, only a handful of flour in a jar and a little oil in a jug. I am gathering a few sticks to take home and make a meal for myself and my son, that we may eat it and die."

Elijah said to her, "Don't be afraid. Go home and do as you have said. But first make a small cake of bread for me from what you have and bring it to me, and then make something for yourself and your son. For this is what the LORD, the God of Israel, says: 'The jar of flour will not be used up and the jug of oil will not run dry until the day the LORD gives rain on the land.'" She went away and did as Elijah had commanded her. Thus began a miracle that lasted for the rest of the famine. Every time she cooked, her jug of oil and her jar of flour remained full. Because of her small offering, the woman, her son, and Elijah had plenty to eat (1 Kings 17).

**80. God really cares about you.**

God loved this widow so much that He asked His servant to walk from the brook of Kerith to the city of Zarephath, a journey of one hundred and thirty miles. On foot it must have taken Elijah five days to bring this woman her miracle.

**81. God does not need you to meet the needs of the man of God; you need the man of God to help you get your needs met.**

Recently I read a secular news report which attacked a man of God. The reporter found a widow living on a fixed income who had given a few dollars to his ministry. Her act of love and faith became a weapon used to accuse the minister of preying on the poor and weak. The same criticism could have been leveled against the prophet Elijah when he asked the widow for her last meal.

In this story Elijah was not the one who needed a miracle. The birds had fed him for over a year. If birds are bringing you burgers (I am translating the raven's bread and meat into modern terms), you do not need to steal a widow's last meal.

The widow was the one who desperately required a miracle. She was down to the bottom of the barrel. She had no options left. Her situation was hopeless. Without a miracle, both she and her son were going to die. So God sent Elijah to her house to help her find her miracle. God did not just send Elijah to get fed, God sent Elijah so the woman could be fed. The point was not to give the prophet a meal, but to give the widow an answer to her problems.

So why did she have to give her last meal before receiving a miracle? Why didn't Elijah solve her problem and then ask for a meal? The answer to this question is obvious. Before God can send a harvest, a seed must be planted. God must have a seed to work with.

**82. Ministers should let God's instructions guide them, not personal need.**

Elijah obeyed an instruction from God. God said to Elijah, *"Go at once to Zarephath of Sidon and stay there. I have commanded a widow in that place to supply you with food"* (1 Kings 17:9).

Elijah was excited because he went from being a lone ranger to having a ministry partner.

**83. If what you have in your hand is not enough to live on, then it must be a seed.**

So Elijah went to Zarephath. *"When he came to the town gate, a widow was there gathering sticks. He called to her and asked, 'Would you bring me a little water in a jar so I may have a drink?' As she was going to get it, he called, 'And bring me, please, a piece of bread'"* (1 Kings 17:10-11).

The widow only had enough food for one meal, then she planned to die. Elijah's request gave her a choice. She could reject him and eat the last thing she has left to give or she could demonstrate her faith by planting a seed into his life. It looks like a hard choice, but she really had nothing to lose. The woman and her son were going to die anyway, eating her seed only delayed her death by a few hours. Her hope for a miracle was greater than her need for a meal.

**84. Everyone, even the poorest, have something in hand which can become a harvest.**

The widow said to Elijah, *"...I have not a cake..."* (1 Kings 17:12 KJV). Jerry Savelle says, "God will change your 'I have not' into 'I have plenty.'" When you feel you have nothing to give, you still have something you can plant. One man had nothing, then he remembered he had a pencil in his pocket. He broke it in half and gave the eraser to God. Now he is a preacher who reaches thousands.

Look around you and find something you can plant. If you have nothing but time, give your time to help someone. Plant something, so that God can release a harvest.

**85. Fear is like a locust, it will eat your harvest before you have it in your hand.**

Elijah said to her, *"Don't be afraid..."* (1 Kings 17:13).

**86. A harvest is most needed during a time of lack.**

Why did God ask this woman with so little to give so much? Because she was the one who needed a miracle the most. Giving takes you from never enough to more than enough!

**87. Every harvest is preceeded by an instruction from God.**

*"...Go home and do as you have said. But first make a small cake of bread for me from what you have and bring it to me, and then make something for yourself and your son"* (1 Kings 17:13).

Jerry Savelle finds the following truths in this passage:

1. In order to release your harvest, you need a prophetic word from God. The best way to get a prophetic word is to spend private time with God.

2. You need to act on your prophetic word from God. This requires obedience on your part. Don't try to rationalize or argue with what God says.

3. You must sow a significant seed. Don't just tip God or sow a token. What is a significant seed? Significant means it has special meaning to you. Ultimately, your life is your most significant seed.

**88. Every request to give should be accompanied by the promise of a harvest.**

*"For this is what the LORD, the God of Israel, says: 'The jar of flour will not be used up and the jug of oil will not run dry until the day the LORD gives rain on the land'"* (1 Kings 17:14). Every instruction is accompanied by a promise. Never ask for an offering without promising a harvest. The promise of the harvest provides the giver with something to wrap her faith around as she plants her seed.

**89. Obedience to a prophetic word from God unlocks your harvest.**

*"She went away and did as Elijah had told her..."* (I Kings 17:15).

**90. A single seed can produce thousands of harvests.**

*"...So there was food every day for Elijah and for the woman and her family. For the jar of flour was not used up and the jug of oil did not run dry, in keeping with the word of the LORD spoken by Elijah"* (1 Kings 17:15-16). By sowing one meal, the widow reaped thousands of meals. Do the math. If Elijah, the woman, and her son ate three times a day for the remaining two years of the famine, the barrel produced 6,570 meals.

**91. Satan targets great harvesters, but the power of the seed will overcome any attack.**

The devil was so mad about the miracle of the bottomless barrel that he attacked the woman's son. The boy died. Elijah took the boy in his arms and cried, *"O LORD my God, let this boy's life return to him!"* Miraculously, he came back to life (see 1 Kings 17:17-23).

*"Then the woman said to Elijah, 'Now I know that you are a man of God and that the word of the LORD from your mouth is the truth'"* (1 Kings 17:24). Humans are so skeptical. Even with the daily miracle of the bottomless barrel, this woman was not fully convinced Elijah was a man of God until her boy was raised from the dead.

**I am not trying to get money FROM you, I am trying to get money TO you!**

When I preach on giving, inevitably someone gets upset and thinks I am just trying to get their money. I explain, "I am not looking for you to give to me. You are not my source. God is my Source. My needs will never be met by your giving, my needs can only be met by my giving. I already know my needs are met because I have a lot of seed in the ground. My harvest is coming whether you put your dollar bill in the offering or not."

# Secrets of the Seed From the Widow in Debt

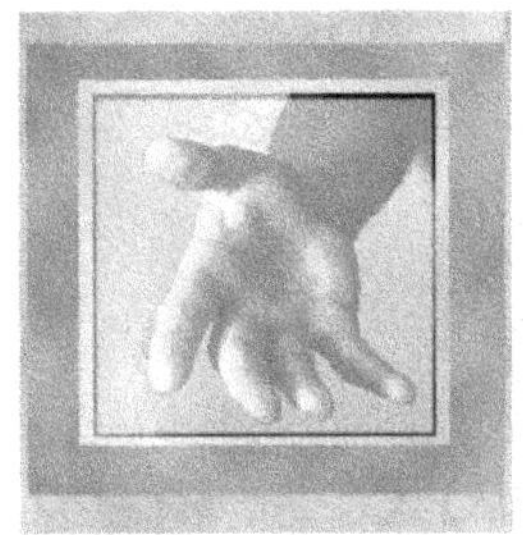

**92. If you want to break free from the bondage of debt, obey the instructions of the man of God.**

*"The wife of a man from the company of the prophets cried out to Elisha, 'Your servant my husband is dead, and you know that he revered the LORD. But now his creditor is coming to take my two boys as his slaves.' Elisha replied to her, 'How can I help you? Tell me, what do you have in your house?' 'Your servant has nothing there at all,' she said, 'except a little oil.' Elisha said, 'Go around and ask all your neighbors for empty jars. Don't ask for just a few. Then go inside and shut the door behind you and your sons. Pour oil into all the jars, and as each is filled, put it to one side.' She left him and afterward shut the door behind her and her sons. They brought the jars to her and she kept pouring. When all the jars were full, she said to her son, 'Bring me another one.' But he replied, 'There is not a jar left.' Then the oil stopped flowing. She went and told the man of God, and he said, 'Go, sell the oil and pay your debts. You and your sons can live on what is left'"* (2 Kings 4:1-7).

**93. Every financial miracle involves a combination of work and supernatural increase.**

This woman used several business principles in receiving her miracle. First, she had to borrow pots from her neighbors. The more pots she borrowed, the more oil she received. Second, she had to work pouring oil from her one pot into the others. Third, she had to go out and sell the oil. The better she was at selling, the more money she had to pay off her debts. Fourth, she had to budget her money so she could continue to live on what was left.

God provided her increase, but she had to work too. As Benjamin Franklin said, "God helps those who help themselves."

# <u>Secrets of the Seed</u>
# From the Kings

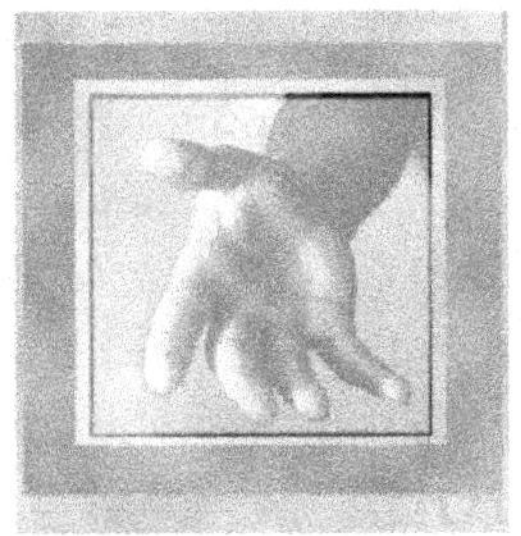

**94. Trust the words of the man of God.**

How do you develop 20/20 vision? Obey 2 Chronicles 20:20, *"Believe in the LORD your God, so shall ye be established; <u>believe His prophets, so shall ye prosper</u>"* (KJV).

**95. Obedience to God is more important than following through on your own plans.**

When King Amaziah went to battle against the country of Edom (2 Chronicles 25), he hired one hundred thousand soldiers from Israel to help fight. But a man of God came to him and said, *"O king, these troops from Israel must not march with you, for the LORD is not with Israel...Even if you go and fight courageously in battle, God will overthrow you before the enemy, for God has the power to help or to overthrow."* Amaziah asked the man of God, 'But what about the hundred talents I paid for these Israelite troops?' The man of God replied, 'The LORD can give you much more than that.' If you obey God, He will compensate you far beyond any temporary loss you may experience.

**96. When you seek God, you prosper; when you stop seeking God, your prosperity becomes meaningless.**

"[King Uzziah] *sought God in the days of Zechariah...and as long as he sought the LORD, God made him to prosper"* (2 Chronicles 26:5 - KJV). Uzziah became king at the age of sixteen and he reigned for fifty-two years. After David and Solomon, he was perhaps the greatest king in Judah's history. As long as he followed the instructions of Zechariah, the priest of God, he had great success. He defeated Judah's enemies and rebuilt many towns that had been destroyed. His fame spread because of his power. He fortified the walls of Jerusalem. He had fields, vineyards, and many livestock, and he had a large well-armed army. Yet after many years of prosperity, he disobeyed the Lord's commands and caught leprosy. His story has a sad ending because his heart filled with pride and he stopped seeking God. This is an important warning for those who are prospering to continue to seek God.

**97. Confidence in God's ability to prosper you will allow you to work in the face of opposition.**

Nehemiah planned to rebuild the walls of Jerusalem, but a group of enemies were mocking him and saying the project could never be completed. Nehemiah replied to their criticism, *"The God of heaven, He will prosper us; therefore we His servants will arise and build"* (Nehemiah 2:20 - KJV). In only fifty-two days, the entire wall was finished.

# Secrets of the Seed From Job

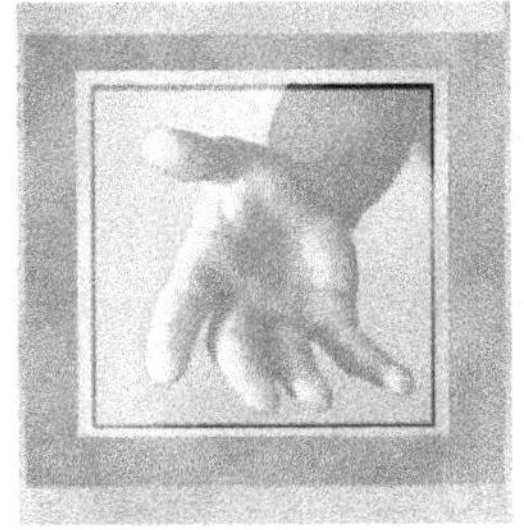

**98.If you sow evil, you will reap evil.**

*"...Those who plow evil and those who sow trouble reap it"* (Job 4:8).

**99. Your future blessings are much greater than your present circumstances.**

*"Your beginnings will seem humble, so prosperous will your future be"* (Job 8:7).

**100. If you participate in God's economy, gold will be more plentiful than dust in your house.**

*"Then shalt thou lay up gold as dust..."* (Job 22:24 - KJV). After you dust a room, three days later the dust has returned. This is what it means to have gold like dust. No matter how much money you spend, it keeps coming back.

**101. The smart seed-sower knows obedience to God is the key to lifelong prosperity.**

*"If they obey and serve Him, they will spend the rest of their days in prosperity and their years in contentment"* (Job 36:11).

**102. When Satan steals, God will restore double.**

*"The LORD blessed the latter part of Job's life more than the first"* (Job 42:12).

**Satan tries to DIVIDE you, the world wants to SUBTRACT from your wealth, you endeavor to ADD to your net worth, but God wants to MULTIPLY you.**

John Tasch, my pastor when I was a child, taught me this illustration which I have used frequently to demonstrate how God wants to multiply our net worth.

I hold up a sheet of paper and ask the audience, "How many corners does this piece of paper have?"

"1-2-3-4," counts the audience.

I say, "What happens if God tells me to give one of my corners away? The typical human response is to say, 'But God, I only have four corners. Could you ask someone else to give who has more corners?' God speaks to me again, 'Daniel, give one of your corners away to the pastor sitting in the front row.'

Reluctantly, I use scissors to cut off one of my corners and hand it over. I ask the pastor who now has the triangle of paper (my former corner) to hold it up in the air. I ask the audience to count how many corners that person has.

"1-2-3," counts the audience.

"Wow," I exclaim, "I gave one corner away, and now this man has three corners. It is a miracle! God has multiplied my corner. It requires great humbleness to give because by giving, you are acknowledging that your money is worth more in the hands of someone else than it is in your hands." I ask the people to count how many corners I have left now that I have given one away.

"1-2-3-4-5."

"Amazing! I started with four corners, gave away one corner, now pastor has three corners, and I still have five corners left."

God speaks, "Give away another corner."

I complain, "But I only have five corners."

God asks in a booming voice, "Who do you think gave you your corners anyway?"

I am starting to figure out how this multiplying stuff works so I cut off another corner and give it to the pastor's wife. I ask the two recipients of my corners to hold them up in the air. "Let's count," I say, "the first triangle has 1-2-3 corners plus the second triangle has 4-5-6 corners." Then I hold up my paper, "How many corners do I have left?"

"1-2-3-4-5-6."

"This is how God's kingdom works. I started with four corners, gave away two, God multiplied it in their hands to become six corners and I still have six corners left. No matter how many corners I give away, the number of corners I have left are multiplied. If you truly believe the Bible, you will be a giver all the time because the Bible says, "Give and it will be given unto you."

# Secrets of the Seed From the Psalms

**103. God takes pleasure in your prosperity!**

God *"hath pleasure in the prosperity of His servant"* (Psalm 35:27 KJV). This means He takes displeasure in your poverty. When you prosper, God is happy.

Prosperity is having more than enough of everything you need and the ability to get everything you want out of life. Prosperity is far more than simply having money. Prosperity includes good health, happiness, abundant wealth, success, and a loving family.

Someone once said, "The one who has no money is poor, but the one who has nothing but money is poorer." As Henry Ward Beecher wrote, "It is the heart that makes a man rich. He is rich according to what he is, not according to what he has." As long as you have what you need (emotionally, spiritually, socially, financially, and materially), you are prosperous.

Prosperity is available to every person on earth who wants it. Your age does not matter. Your level of education does not matter. Where you live does not matter. The economic conditions around you do not matter because prosperity is possible in both good times and bad times. It does not matter who you know or how much money you have right now.

You can become prosperous by following God's laws of seed-time and harvest. For thousands of years farmers have been sowing seed and reaping harvests. They understand the principle that whatever seed you sow will grow and over time will produce a harvest. These same principles apply to every area of life. The principles of seedtime and harvest apply equally to the realms of farming, business, spiritual growth, relationships, and family life.

**104. The smart seed-sower knows God never forgets His own.**

*"I was young and now I am old, yet I have never seen the righteous forsaken or their children begging bread"* (Psalm 37:25).

**105. Those who are planted (and who plant) in the house of the Lord shall thrive.**

*"The righteous will flourish like a palm tree, they will grow like a cedar of Lebanon; planted in the house of the LORD, they will flourish in the courts of our God. They will still bear fruit in old age, they will stay fresh and green"* (Psalm 92:12-14). It is important to stay planted in the house of the Lord where there is an abundance of water, sunlight (Son-light), fertilizer, pruning, and nurture. If you are transplanted away from heaven's oasis, you will dry up and turn brown. But, if you remain planted in God's court you will stay green and continue to grow and bear fruit year after year.

**106. Those who are sad when they give will become glad when they receive.**

*"They that sow in tears shall reap in joy"* (Psalm 126:5 KJV). Have you ever put money in the offering and asked yourself "What in the world did I just do?" The Bible says, *"God loves a cheerful giver"* (2 Corinthians 9:7), but Mike Murdock points out that God does not hate an uncheerful giver. It is easy to have giver's remorse, but God promises that even if you are crying while you are giving you will be joyful when you receive.

Often, immediately after I plant a seed, I become depressed

because of the size of my gift. Questions run through my mind. What was I thinking? How am I going to pay my bills? Why did I give so much? But later, as I start to receive a harvest on the seed, I start asking myself, "Why didn't I give more?" *"He who goes out weeping, carrying seed to sow, will return with songs of joy, carrying sheaves with him"* (Psalm 126:6).

**107. Praise proceeds harvest.**

*"...O God; may all the peoples praise You. Then the land will yield its harvest, and God, our God, will bless us"* (Psalm 67:5-6).

**108. Your promotion is not in the hands of your boss, it is in the hands of the Lord.**

*"For promotion cometh neither from the east, nor from the west, nor from the south. But God is the Judge: He putteth down one, and setteth up another"* (Psalm 75:6 KJV). God gave you your job. It is He who promotes you.

**109. The harvest comes from the Lord.**

*"The LORD will indeed give what is good, and our land will yield its harvest"* (Psalm 85:12).

**110. An openhanded giver is able to receive, but a closed fist blocks God's abundance.**

When God gives, He is an openhanded giver. As the psalmist said, *"You open your hand and satisfy the desires of every living thing"* (Psalm 145:16). We should give the same way. If your hand is open, you can receive. But if your hand is balled up into a fist, not only can you not give, you can't receive either.

Hold your hand in front of you right now. Make a fist. Imagine God is trying to pour blessings into your hand. How many of those blessings will you be able to keep if you have a closed fist? Now, unfold your hand in front of you so you can see your open palm. Obviously, it is much easier to receive from God when your palm is visible. Every Sunday should be "Palm" Sunday, not just the Sunday before Easter.

**You cannot take money with you to heaven, but you can send it on ahead.**

A man died and went to heaven. He was met at the pearly gates by St. Peter who led him down the golden streets. They walked past mansion after beautiful mansion until they came to the end of the street where they stopped in front of a cardboard shack. The man asked St. Peter why he got a hut when there were so many mansions he could live in. St. Peter replied, "We did the best we could with the money you sent us."

# <u>Secrets of the Seed</u>
# From Proverbs

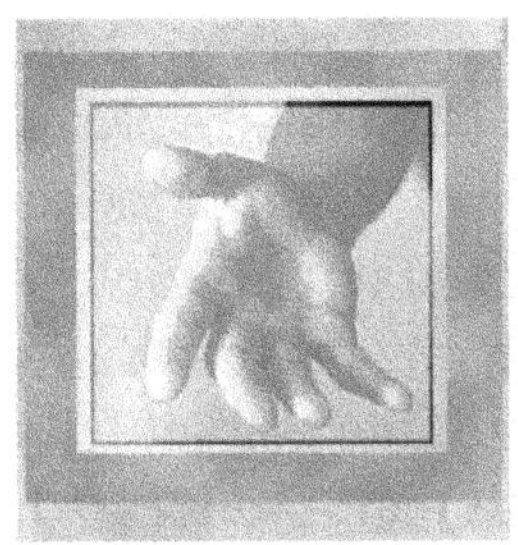

**111. The foolish quickly lose their wealth.**

*"...the prosperity of fools shall destroy them"* (Proverbs 1:32 KJV). It is possible God has not been able to bless you the way He wants to because you are still learning how to handle money. If you think this might be your problem, start asking God for wisdom (James 1:5). Educate yourself financially. Understand how money can work for you. Learn about the rewards of investing and the pain of unpaid debts. Ask someone who is rich how they became wealthy and how they stay wealthy. Once you have the wisdom to handle wealth, God can begin to bless you.

**112. Giving to God is a great way to acknowledge your dependence upon Him.**

*"In all your ways acknowledge Him, and He will make your paths straight"* (Proverbs 3:6). You should always honor God first, then He will direct your steps down the best path for your life.

**113. The smart seed-sower knows that giving money to God is a way to honor Him.**

*"Honor the LORD with your wealth, with the firstfruits of all your crops; then your barns will be filled to overflowing, and your vats will brim over with new wine"* (Proverbs 3:9-10). When you honor God with your firstfruits (tithes), God will honor you by causing your bank accounts (modern day barns) to overflow.

**114. Those who love God find enduring wealth, not the illusion of prosperity that can disappear overnight.**

*"I love those who love Me....With Me are riches and honor, enduring wealth and prosperity....I walk in the way of righteousness... bestowing wealth on those who love Me and making their treasuries full"* (Proverbs 8:17-21). Statistics prove that many people who win the lottery or inherit a large sum of money lose all the money within a couple of years and end up in serious debt. During the "dot com" boom, investors made huge sums of money on paper but then lost it all when the bottom of the market fell out. But God does not give you the kind of wealth that disappears in a puff of smoke. No, He gives enduring, long lasting wealth. In other words, He makes your treasuries full and gives you the wisdom to know how to keep them full.

**115. The harvest often comes disguised as hard work and those who are lazy will lose out.**

*"He who gathers crops in summer is a wise son, but he who sleeps during harvest is a disgraceful son"* (Proverbs 10:5).

**116. You can be rich without following God's guidelines, but you can't be happy.**

There are many kinds of wealth which give nothing but trouble. God gives you wealth free from problems. "*The blessing of the LORD brings wealth, and He adds no trouble to it"* (Proverbs 10:22).

**117. The more you give, the more you have; the more you hoard, the less you have.**

*"One man gives freely, yet gains even more; another withholds unduly, but comes to poverty. A generous man will prosper; he who refreshes others will himself be refreshed"* (Proverbs 11:24-25). The King James Version reads, *"The liberal soul shall be made fat..."* (Proverbs 11:25). "Fat" means abundance. What does it mean to have a liberal soul? *"But the liberal deviseth liberal things; and by liberal things shall he stand"* (Isaiah 32:8 KJV).

Jesus talked about the liberal soul when He said, *"If someone wants to sue you and take your tunic, let him have your cloak as well. If someone forces you to go one mile, go with him two miles. Give to the one who asks you, and do not turn away from the one who wants to borrow from you"* (Matthew 5:40-42). The liberal soul gives more than is asked for, goes farther than required, and gives to all who ask.

**118. Confession of God's promises brings possession of God's promises.**

*"From the fruit of his lips a man is filled with good things as surely as the work of his hands rewards him"* (Proverbs 12:14). Every word you speak is a seed of either good or evil.

**119. You cannot leave a financial inheritance to your grandchildren unless you are wealthy.**

*"A good man leaves an inheritance for his children's children..."* (Proverbs 13:22)

**120. Sowing releases the world's wealth into the hands of believers.**

*"...The wealth of the sinner is laid up for the just"* (Proverbs 13:22 -- KJV). If the world does not use wealth properly, it reverts to the righteous by default. This idea is echoed in Job 27:13-17 *"Here is the fate God allots to the wicked, the heritage a ruthless man receives from the Almighty...his offspring will never have enough to eat... Though he heaps up silver like dust and clothes like piles of clay, what he lays up the righteous will wear, and the innocent will divide his silver."*

Here are some examples of the wealth of the wicked being transferred to the pockets of the righteous:

* When Abraham arrived in Egypt he was relatively poor, but when he left, Pharaoh had made him rich (Genesis 12:16).

* When Jacob arrived at Laban's house, he was dirt-poor, but by the time he left, Laban's flocks and herds had made him wealthy (Genesis 31:9).

* When the children of Israel left Egypt, they took the wealth of the Egyptians with them (Exodus 12:36).

* When Elijah was fed by the ravens, where did the food come from? I like to think the birds stole it from the wicked King Ahab's table (1 Kings 17).

*Peter went fishing and found money in the mouth of a fish. The coin probably dropped out of a wicked man's pocket during a boat ride and a fish brought it to Peter (Matthew 17:24-27).

You do not necessarily inherit the world's wealth because of anything good you do, but because of the former owners misuse of the money. God said to the Israelites right before they moved into the promised land, *"It is not because of your righteousness or your integrity that you are going in to take possession of their land; but on account of the wickedness of these nations, the LORD your God will drive them out before you..."* (Deuteronomy 9:5).

However, be warned, if you do not use the wealth God has given you properly, you will lose it just as surely as the wicked lost it. "*Like the nations the LORD destroyed before you, so you will be destroyed for not obeying the LORD your God"* (Deuteronomy 8:20).

**121. The giving of the wicked is detested by God.**

*"The LORD detests the sacrifice of the wicked..."* (Proverbs 15:8).

**122. Your giving creates a harvest of favor for you among the great.**

*"A man's gift maketh room for him, and bringeth him before great men"* (Proverbs 18:16 KJV). The smart seed-sower knows giving opens many doors of opportunity.

**123. The generous seed sower will have many friends.**

*"...Everyone is the friend of a man who gives gifts"* (Proverbs 19:6). This verse does not mean you buy friends with your money, but it does mean your giving creates an appeal that draws people to you.

**124. Giving to the poor is lending to the Lord.**

*"He who is kind to the poor lends to the LORD, and He will reward him for what he has done"* (Proverbs 19:17). When you sow into the life of a needy person, God assumes the responsibility for giving you a harvest.

**125. If you refuse to plant, you schedule a season of lack.**

*"A sluggard does not plow in season; so at harvest time he looks but finds nothing"* (Proverbs 20:4). Mike Murdock explains, "A seed of nothing guarantees a season of nothing."

**126. You must give God something to work with.**

Oral Roberts said, "You must put something in if you want to get something out." He used the illustration of putting a coin into a vending machine. It would be unreasonable to expect a can of soda from the machine if you have not put anything into the coin slot.

The number "0" when multiplied by any other number produces the sum of zero. If you give God nothing, and He multiplies your nothing by 30, 60, or 100 fold, you still end up with nothing. God can not multiply "0." Oral Roberts says, "You must give God something to work with."

The seed releases God's "super" on our "natural," but if we do not do our part, God cannot do His part. When we do our part in the natural realm, God is able to do His part in the supernatural realm. But if we have not done what we are supposed to do in the natural, how can God bless us?

**127. A secret seed will stop anger that is directed against you.**

*"A gift given in secret soothes anger..."* (Proverbs 21:14). If someone is angry with you, send them a gift. It is hard to explain

but even if they do not know you sent the gift, this often causes their anger to dissipate.

**128. Poverty is a tragedy.**

*"The rich rule over the poor, and the borrower is servant to the lender"* (Proverbs 22:7).

Here are some reasons not to be poor:

* The poor will forever be enslaved to the whims of their creditors.

* The poor miss the opportunity to be significant givers. It is better to be a giver than a receiver. Those living in poverty will always be receivers with their hands stretched out and will never experience the greater joy of giving.

* The poor fail to do their part to complete the Great Commission.

* The poor can never solve anyone's problems. You cannot help others if you need help yourself. The best thing you can do for the poor is to not be one of them.

* The poor are trapped by the "rat race" of paying this month's bills. They rarely have time to set aside for prayer, fasting, studying God's word, or going on mission trips.

**129. Generous seed sowing ensures a future of plenty.**

*"A generous man will himself be blessed, for he shares his food with the poor"* (Proverbs 22:9).

**130. There is a right way and a wrong way to accumulate wealth.**

Godly ways of increasing wealth are based upon the principles of giving. Ungodly ways of amassing wealth rely upon taking. Proverbs 28:8 warns that those who take will ultimately be forced to give all they have to another who has followed God's way. *"He who increases his wealth by exorbitant interest amasses it for another, who will be kind to the poor."* The wealth of the wicked is laid up for the righteous or as I like to put it "the wealth of the takers is reserved for the givers."

**131. The difference between a blessed life and a cursed life is your seed.** *"He who gives to the poor will lack nothing, but he who closes his eyes to them receives many curses"* (Proverbs 28:27).

# Secrets of the Seed From Ecclesiastes

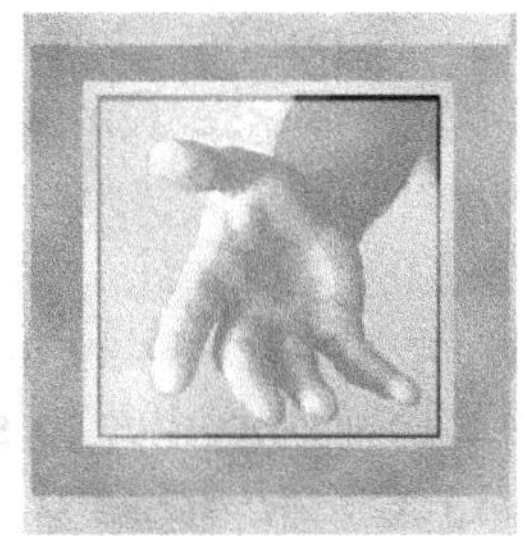

**132. Do not let circumstances, excuses, doubts, or skepticism prevent you from sowing.**

*"Whoever watches the wind will not plant; whoever looks at the clouds will not reap"* (Ecclesiastes 11:4). If your eyes are on your circumstances instead of on God, you will miss the chance to sow and you will miss your opportunity to reap. Like the wind, doubts blow through skeptical minds; like the clouds, circumstances create excuses for not sowing. What are some of the clouds and winds of negative voices which could prevent your harvest?

**133. Giving is God's antidote for greed.**

Greed ruins lives. Satan was cast from heaven because he became greedy for more power than he was intended to have. Adam and Eve lost their relationship with God because of a greed for unauthorized knowledge. Judas betrayed Jesus because greed controlled his soul.

What is the difference between a spirit of greed and a spirit of generosity? Greed is the desire to have more than what you deserve. Generosity is the desire to give more than you can afford. Greed wants something for nothing. Generosity gives something to someone else who has nothing. Greed takes. Generosity gives.

Giving proves the cancer of greed has been eliminated in your life. If you are willing to give away anything you own, then what you have will never control you.

Greed should never be the motivation for giving. You do not give just to get. You give for the sake of giving and you receive for the sake of being able to give more. If your motivation for giving is greed, then God will not honor your giving.

Greed is never satisfied. No matter what a greedy man owns, he always desires more. As wise King Solomon said, *"Whoever loves money never has money enough; whoever loves wealth is never satisfied with his income..."* (Ecclesiastes 5:10).

Two brothers were fighting over an inheritance. One of them asked Jesus to force the other brother to split the money with him. Jesus said to them, *"Watch out! Be on your guard against all kinds of greed; a man's life does not consist in the abundance of his possessions"* (Luke 12:15).

If all you want is things then you have a greed problem. If you have a greed problem, start giving your things away and your problem will be cured really quick. Some critics say seed-faith principles lead to greed in the church. But this is not true. Giving to get does not work very long because the greedy do not give and givers quickly overcome inner covetousness.

Your life is not judged by what you own, but by what you give. Material things are ultimately just "stuff" that gets in the way. I relearn this lesson every time I move. As I sort through piles of junk trying to decide what to keep, what to throw away, and the best way to store a souvenir so it will not break, I realize how useless and meaningless most material possessions are. The best way to eliminate greed is to make a deal with God that you are willing to give away anything you own if God tells you to do so.

There is no problem owning nice cars, expensive watches, and big houses as long as you recognize that you do not really own them,

God does. He gave them to you, and He should be able to ask you to give them to one of His other servants. You only truly own what you give away. If you cannot find the inner strength to give something away, then you no longer own that possession, it owns you.

Our focus should be on heavenly treasure, instead of earthly possessions. *"Since, then, you have been raised with Christ, set your hearts on things above, where Christ is seated at the right hand of God"* (Colossians 3:1).

**134. Keep sowing consistently because you never know which seed will produce the greatest harvest.**

*"Sow your seed in the morning, and at evening let not your hands be idle, for you do not know which will succeed, whether this or that, or whether both will do equally well"* (Ecclesiastes 11:6). One day a man asked the millionaire H.L. Hunt how much money he spent every year on advertising. He replied, "Two million dollars." The man asked now much of that advertising budget did him any good. Mr. Hunt answered, "About half." The man then asked, "Why not cut out the half that does not help?" Hunt responded, "I would if I knew which half worked."

Different types of ground produce different size harvests. Until you get the wisdom of the Holy Spirit concerning where you can maximize your harvest, it is important to continue sowing seed in a variety of fields.

## Eleven Elements Affecting Your Harvests

1. Quality of seed — Exodus 12:5
   Are you giving your best to God?
2. Amount of seed — 2 Corinthians 9:6
   Are you giving enough to God?
3. Type of seed — Galatians 6:7
   Are you sowing a seed of what you have a need of?
4. Quality of the soil — Mark 4:8
   Are you sowing into good ground?
5. The season you are in — Jeremiah 5:24
   Are you in a period of sowing, growing, or reaping?
6. Expectation of the sower — Mark 11:24
   What is your faith level for the seed you are sowing?
7. Need of the sower — Psalm 37:25
   Are your basic needs being met?
8. Heart of the sower — Acts 5:1-11
   Are your motives right?
9. Behavior of the sower — Haggai 1:5-7
   Are your actions right?
10. Weeds in the garden — Hebrews 12:15
    Have you repented of sin?
11. Work of the enemy — Mark 4:8
    Have you rebuked Satan?

# Secrets of the Seed From Isaiah

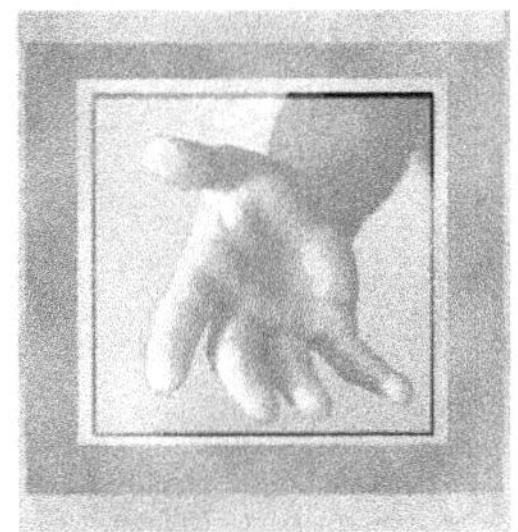

**135. Your attitude towards sowing is as important as the action of sowing.**

*"If you are willing and obedient, you will eat the best from the land..."* (Isaiah 1:19). Being willing has to do with your emotions, and being obedient has to do with your actions. It is possible to be obedient to God's commands without being mentally willing.

Some people tithe because they have to, not because they want to. But for God, the attitude with which you do something is as important as the action of doing it. This is why *"God loves a cheerful giver"* (2 Corinthians 9:7). If it mentally hurts you to put your money in the offering on Sunday, if you agonize all week about it, if you get mad when the preacher mentions giving, why don't you just keep your dollar?

If we listen to God, He will teach us how to sow, when to sow, and what to sow (Isaiah 28:23-29).

**136. The rain which causes your seed to grow comes from God.**

*"He will also send you rain for the seed you sow in the ground, and the food that comes from the land will be rich and plentiful..."* (Isaiah 30:23).

**137. Growth is a process.**

This verse reveals that there are cycles of sowing and reaping. *"This year you will eat what grows by itself, and the second year what springs from that. But in the third year sow and reap, plant vineyards and eat their fruit"* (Isaiah 37:30). If you are only planting a couple of dollars in the offering, you cannot expect to receive a harvest of millions of dollars. You must build to that level of receiving. Plant what you can and when you receive a harvest, plant again. As you plant more and more seed, your harvests will continually grow.

**138. God restores harvests that have been lost.**

*"Once more a remnant of the house of Judah will take root below and bear fruit above"* (Isaiah 37:31).

**139. Treasures that have been hidden in secret hiding places will be harvested by those whom God loves.**

*"I will give you the treasures of darkness, riches stored in secret places, so that you may know that I am the LORD, the God of Israel, who summons you by name"* (Isaiah 45:3).

**140. God's classroom is better than earning an MBA from the top business school in the nation.**

If you listen, God will teach you how to profit. *"Thus saith the LORD, thy Redeemer, the Holy One of Israel; I am the LORD thy God which teacheth thee to profit, which leadeth thee by the way that thou shouldest go"* (Isaiah 48:17 KJV).

**141. Giving away what you've <u>got</u> to get what you've <u>not</u> got doesn't make sense in the natural, but it does in God's economy.**

God says, *"'For My thoughts are not your thoughts, neither are your ways My ways,' declares the LORD. 'As the heavens are higher than the earth, so are My ways higher than your ways and My thoughts than your thoughts'"* (Isaiah 55:8). At first glance, God's way of doing things does not make sense. Logic tells us to hoard, not to give. It is hard to wrap our human brains around the idea that a tiny seed can produce a massive harvest. But God does not operate according to the dictates of human logic, He works in ways we will never understand.

## Excuses People Give for NOT Expecting a Harvest

No one gets mad when you talk about giving until you start talking about receiving.

"There is nothing I need."
"God wants us to be poor."
"I don't give just to get."
"God is not a slot machine."
"I'm too holy to need things."
"I can wait until heaven to be blessed."
"I don't need God's help, I can survive by myself."
"What will people think if God starts blessing me?"
"I don't want to be perceived as greedy,
I want everyone to think I have pure motives."
"Promises about harvests are just
another way for preachers to get my money."
"I gave before and nothing happened,
I don't expect anything this time either."
"God already gave us infinite riches when He provided for our salvation...it is presumptuous to ask Him for anything more."

# Secrets of the Seed From Jeremiah

**142. The smart seed-sower remembers to fear God, the One who guarantees the harvest.**

*"...Let us fear the LORD our God, who gives autumn and spring rains in season, who assures us of the regular weeks of harvest"* (Jeremiah 5:24).

**143. Sin's punishment is the loss of the harvest.**

To those who do evil, worship false idols, cling to deceit, refuse to repent, ignore God's direction, misinterpret Scripture, and reject the Word, the Lord declares, *"I will take away their harvest... There will be no grapes on the vine. There will be no figs on the tree, and their leaves will wither. What I have given them will be taken from them"* (Jeremiah 8:13).

**144. God mapped out your road to prosperity.**

*"'For I know the plans I have for you,' declares the LORD, 'plans to prosper you and not to harm you, plans to give you hope and a future'"* (Jeremiah 29:11).

**145. If we do not do our part in winning souls, we will be held responsible for their loss.**

*"When I say to a wicked man, 'You will surely die,' and you do not warn him or speak out to dissuade him from his evil ways in order to save his life, that wicked man will die for his sin, and I will hold you accountable for his blood. But if you do warn the wicked man and he does not turn from his wickedness or from his evil ways, he will die for his sin; but you will have saved yourself"* (Ezekiel 3:18-19). It is not our responsibility to bring all people to Christ, but to bring Christ to all people.

**The seed is stronger than concrete.**

I was walking down a sidewalk when I saw a tiny plant pushing its way up through the concrete. When the contractors laid the sidewalk, it looked like a hopeless situation for the seed. But the persistence of the seed was greater than the negative situation of hardened concrete. Sometimes, it may feel like Satan has poured concrete over your seeds. But, the seed is more powerful than concrete.

# Secrets of the Seed From Hosea

**146. We are destroyed by lack of knowledge, not lack of money.**

*"...my people are destroyed from lack of knowledge"* (Hosea 4:6). This idea is echoed in Isaiah 5:13, *"Therefore my people are gone into captivity, because they have no knowledge..."* (KJV).

**147. God has appointed a harvest for you.**

*"Also for you, Judah, a harvest is appointed"* (Hosea 6:11).

**148. If you sow righteousness, you will reap love.**

*"Sow for yourselves righteousness, reap the fruit of unfailing love, and break up your unplowed ground; for it is time to seek the LORD, until He comes and showers righteousness on you"* (Hosea 10:12). Notice, in this verse, the importance of plowing your ground is emphasized.

## Be a go-giver, not a go-getter in life.

Brian Tracy talks about being a "go-giver" instead of a "go-getter." Don't live with the attitude, "What's in it for me?" Try not to be a taker in life, make a decision to be a giver. We should live to give, not live to get. Robb Thompson says, "Don't need a lot, be a lot."

Do not be focused only on yourself. Selfishness is the greatest enemy of prosperity. Don't sit around feeling sorry for yourself, look for someone you can help. Do what you can do. Mow someone's lawn. Give a friend a ride. Buy your wife a present. Tip a little more generously. Give extra in the offering. Go the extra mile at work. Speak an encouraging word.

If we are always taking, we become constipated, bloated, and puffed-up, but giving keeps us healthy. A good illustration of this concept is the difference between the Dead Sea and the Sea of Galilee in the land of Israel. The Dead Sea has water coming into it but no outlet for the water to leave. As the sun evaporates the water, all the sediment is left behind. The salt content of the water is so high that nothing can live in the Dead Sea. The Sea of Galilee, on the other hand, is teeming with fish because water can both enter and leave. Charles Neiman points out, "God is not in the business of building swamps and reservoirs."

# Secrets of the Seed From Joel

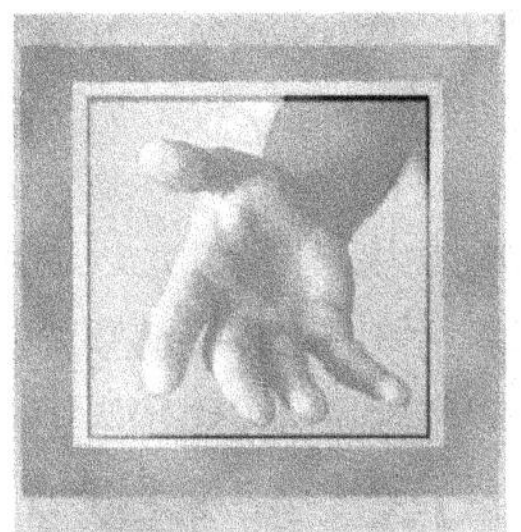

**149. Harvest begins with repentance.**

The chain of events in the second chapter of Joel are worth noting. First comes revival. *"Even now,' declares the LORD, 'return to Me with all your heart, with fasting and weeping and mourning... Blow the trumpet in Zion, declare a holy fast, call a sacred assembly. Gather the people, consecrate the assembly...Let the priests, who minister before the LORD, weep between the temple porch and the altar"* (Joel 2:12-17).

**150. Part of repentance involves planting a seed.**

*"...Leave behind a blessing, grain offerings and drink offerings for the LORD your God..."* (Joel 2:14).

**151. Harvest follows revival.**

*"The LORD replied to them: 'I am sending you grain, new wine and oil, enough to satisfy you fully....the open pastures are becoming green. The trees are bearing their fruit; the fig tree and*

*the vine yield their riches....He sends you abundant showers, both autumn and spring rains, as before. The threshing floors will be filled with grain; the vats will overflow with new wine and oil"* (Joel 2:19,22-24).

**152. God restores the harvests Satan has stolen.**

Next comes restoration. *"I will restore to you the years that the locust hath eaten, the cankerworm, and the caterpillar, and the palmerworm, my great army which I sent among you. And ye shall eat in plenty, and be satisfied, and praise the Name of the LORD your God, that hath dealt wondrously with you: and My people shall never be ashamed"* (Joel 2:25-26 KJV).

Why are locusts, cankerworms, caterpillears, and palmerworms so feared by farmers? Locusts swarm and eat everything in sight. A year's harvest can be wiped out within minutes. Cankerworms burrow tunnels into the stalk of a plant causing it to fall over. Caterpillars chew on the leaves. Palmerworms eat the roots of plants. These bugs represent an all-out assault upon the harvest.

Satan will do anything he can to destroy your harvest because he knows that if he can steal your harvest, you will never have enough seed to plant another crop again. For a long time, Satan has probably been raiding your harvest, but God promises to restore the years of damage caused by Satan's attack. According to this verse, God will "restore" you. He will give back all the harvests Satan has tried to steal and you shall "eat in plenty!" Never again will you be "ashamed" by your lack.

**153. Financial harvest is a predecessor to world harvest.**

Finally, God's Spirit is poured out and world evangelism occurs. *"Afterward, I will pour out My Spirit on all people. Your sons and daughters will prophesy, your old men will dream dreams, your young men will see visions. Even on My servants, both men and women, I will pour out My Spirit in those days....everyone who calls on the Name of the LORD will be saved..."* (Joel 2:28-32).

# Secrets of the Seed From Haggai, Zechariah, & Micah

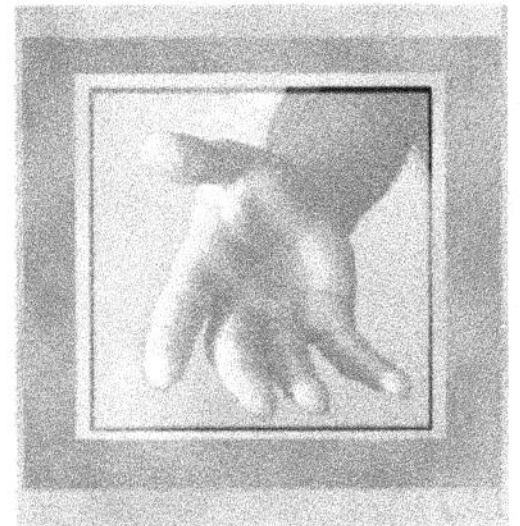

**154. If your harvest is small, consider your ways.**

The dishonesty of the Israelites cost them their harvest. *"Now this is what the LORD Almighty says: 'Give careful thought to your ways. You have planted much, but have harvested little. You eat, but never have enough. You drink, but never have your fill. You put on clothes, but are not warm. You earn wages, only to put them in a purse with holes in it.' This is what the LORD Almighty says: 'Give careful thought to your ways'* (Haggai 1:5-7).

**155. Your seed will grow, your crops will be watered, the ground will produce, and your harvest will come.**

*"The seed will grow well, the vine will yield its fruit, the ground will produce its crops, and the heavens will drop their dew. I will give all these things as an inheritance to the remnant of this people"* (Zechariah 8:12).

**156. The price of disobedience is the loss of your harvest.**

In the sixth chapter of Micah, the Lord builds a legal case against Israel. He points out that He has delivered them from Egypt, the land of slavery. In exchange, He asked them to act justly, and to love mercy, and to walk humbly with God. Yet they have become violent liars who are dishonest in business deals. In judgment, God says, *"You will plant but not harvest; you will press olives but not use the oil on yourselves, you will crush grapes but not drink the wine"* (Micah 6:15).

# Secrets of the Seed Concerning the Tithe

**157. God never changed His mind concerning the tithe.**

*"I the LORD do not change. So you, O descendants of Jacob, are not destroyed"* (Malachi 3:6). God does not change. Newspapers change every day. Circumstances change. People change. But God does not change. Jesus Christ is the same yesterday, today, and forever (Hebrews 13:8). What He did in the past, He will do today!

God's unchangeableness is why He kept His covenant with the Israelites. God gave His word that He would not destroy them and even though they repeatedly made God angry, He kept His word. Why? Because He does not change.

Incidentally, this is a good reason why we should tithe today. Some scholars say the New Testament church does not have to tithe because tithing is commanded under the old law. Since we are free from the law, they say we should not tithe. But this verse tells us that God does not change. If He wanted a tithe in the past, He still wants it today.

It is true that we have been set free from the law, but the

principle of tithing predates the Law of Moses. In Genesis 14:18-20, Abraham tithed to King Melchizedek. We are the children of Abraham, so we should tithe.

**158. Pay your tithe before you do anything else with your money.**

*"Honor the LORD with your wealth, with the firstfruits of all your crops; then your barns will be filled to overflowing, and your vats will brim over with new wine"* (Proverbs 3:9-10). What are the firstfruits of a harvest? They are the first yield of your land. They represent the best of what you have. We should bring the best we have to God.

We should give to God first before doing anything else with our crops. Do not give God the leftovers. The tail end of the harvest is the part used to feed animals.

**159. If you are not tithing, you have drifted away from fully serving God.**

*"'Ever since the time of your forefathers you have turned away from My decrees and have not kept them. Return to Me, and I will return to you,' says the LORD Almighty. 'But you ask, "How are we to return?"'"* (Malachi 3:7).

In this chapter of Malachi, the prophet is putting the children of Israel on trial. Imagine a courtroom scene. God is the Judge and the prosecutor. The Israelites are the defendants. We have peeked in at the point where evidence is being presented which proves that the Israelites have fallen away from God.

Despite their disobedience, God is still giving them a chance to repent. Isn't it awesome that our God is a God of second chances?

If we return to God, He will return to us. In reality, God never went anywhere. We just stepped off the path He was on. If we return to the path, we will be at His side once again.

Like many people, the Israelites want to know how they can return. The first step in returning to God is tithing. Where your money is, there is your heart also.

**160. Failure to tithe is robbing God.**

*"Will a man rob God? Yet you rob Me. But you ask, 'How do*

*we rob You?' In tithes and offerings."* (Malachi 3:8).

In Mexico while I was ushering at a meeting, I observed a curious practice. People would put a large bill in the offering and then take change from the offering bucket. A couple of times I was sure I saw someone taking more change out of the bucket than the amount they had put into the bucket. I have never seen a more blatant example of people robbing God. Thousands of believers would say, "I would never even think about robbing God in such a despicable manner." Yet if you are not paying your tithes, you are robbing God just the same as if you brought a gun to church and literally stole the offering from the ushers. It is preposterous to think that anyone can rob God. How can you steal from an all-knowing, all-powerful Being? He owns the cattle on a thousand hills; have you been rustling a few of His cows? Yet God insists, "you have robbed Me." This statement by the prosecution is hard to swallow. The defense immediately protests and asks "How did we rob God?"

They robbed God by not giving Him His due. In reality, everything we own belongs to God. All God asks for is a tiny tip to prove our thankfulness for His bounty. It's amazing that people will tip a waitress, even a bad waitress, more than they will give to God.

**161. A tithe of all your income belongs to the Lord.**

*"A tithe of everything from the land, whether grain from the soil or fruit from the trees, belongs to the LORD; it is holy to the LORD"* (Leviticus 27:30). The tithe is not something we give God. The tithe already belongs to God. You do not give your tithe, you pay your tithe. Tithing is a debt you owe, giving is a seed you sow. The offering, on the other hand is a freewill offering. You can choose how much you want to give God.

**162. The word "tithe" means ten percent.**

*"The entire tithe of the herd and flock, every tenth animal that passes under the shepherd's rod, will be holy to the LORD"* (Leviticus 27:32). What is the tithe? The word "tithe" means 10%. We are supposed to give God ten percent of everything we earn. You can't tithe 20% of your income, you can only tithe 10%.

Some people get hung up on whether they should tithe on

their net income or their gross income. I think it is up to you how much you want to give to God. Do you want to be blessed on your net giving, or your gross giving?

Should you pay your tithes before or after taxes? Jesus said, *"Give to Caesar what is Caesar's, and to God what is God's"* (Matthew 22:21). If you pay the tithe after you pay your taxes, who are you putting first, the government or God?

Paying the tithe should come before paying your bills. You say, "I can't afford to tithe." The truth is you can't afford not to tithe.

**163. God charges 20% interest on His tithe money.**

*"If a man redeems any of his tithe, he must add a fifth of the value to it"* (Leviticus 27:31). God charges as much interest as credit card companies. If you have not been paying God what you owe Him, you should rectify your mistake quickly.

**164. You cannot sow until you pay what you owe.**

We pay tithes and give offerings. The difference is that you owe the tithe to God and the offering is a gift you give of your own free will. We have to pay the tithe, and we get to give the offering. The tithe is what you owe, the offering is what you sow. You do not give the electric company money, you pay them because you owe a bill. You do not owe your friend a birthday present, you give it to them.

Sowing seed does not make up for failing to pay what you owe. If you owe your mortgage company $700 each month and you send them a $150 check and ask them to use it to pay down the principal, they will not do it until you make the regular monthly payment.

Tithing plows your field, and giving sows your seed. Some Christians try to plant seed before they have plowed the field. Tithing opens the windows of heaven, giving determines the measure God uses to pour blessing out those windows.

**165. Tithing should come first in your budget.**

Statistics show that in most churches twenty percent of the people give eighty percent of the money. This is because most church members know they are supposed to tithe but very few actually do.

Your giving is an indication of your level of commitment to Jesus Christ. The reason not many Christians tithe is because not many Christians are truly committed to God. This means the pews of our churches are full of lukewarm believers. By examining your financial statement for five minutes, you can discover where your true priorities lie. Your checkbook reveals what is important to you.

For millions of Christians the mortgage, car payments, clothes, entertainment, retirement investments, and a family vacation take priority over tithing. After everything else is paid for, the leftovers are given to God. But God desires the firstfruits. Before we budget money for anything else, we should make sure we are giving to God first.

**166. Tithing is our way of thanking God for setting us free from the curse of the law.**

*"You are under a curse, the whole nation of you, because you are robbing Me"* (Malachi 3:9). In Malachi, the entire nation is under a curse for their failure to tithe. But in New Testament times, Jesus set us free from the curse of the law (Galatians 3:13). If we tithe because we are fearful of being under a curse, God cannot bless us because fear is the opposite of faith and only faith pleases God (Hebrews 11:6). Today we tithe, not because the law forces us to tithe, but because we are thankful for what God has done for us.

**167. Tithing opens the windows of heaven over your life.**

*"'Bring the whole tithe into the storehouse, that there may be food in My house. Test Me in this,' says the LORD Almighty, 'and see if I will not throw open the floodgates of heaven and pour out so much blessing that you will not have room enough for it'"* (Malachi 3:10).

What does it mean for the floodgates of heaven to open? We find the answer in Genesis 7:11 during the beginning of Noah's flood. *"In the six hundredth year of Noah's life...all the springs of the great deep burst forth, and <u>the floodgates of the heavens were opened.</u> And rain fell on the earth forty days and forty nights"* (Genesis 7:11-12). Not a trickle, not a stream, not a river, but a flood of blessing!

**168. Your harvest can be bigger than your barns.**

*"...so much blessing that you will not have room enough for it"* (Malachi 3:10). A friend gave me a new color printer for my computer. I was so excited. I rushed home to hook it up only to discover that my desk was too small to fit my new printer. I immediately thought of this verse and started asking God for a bigger desk.

**169. Pay your tithe at the house that feeds you.**

You cannot eat at Burger King, and pay at McDonalds. Give to whoever is feeding your spirit. We are supposed to bring the tithe into God's storehouse. The "storehouse" was the place where God's glory, God's presence, and God's word was in those days. Today the storehouse is your local church where you are fed God's word and experience His presence. This enables the pastor to have food on his or her table. It also allows him to feed others.

Pay your tithe where you are spiritually fed. If you are sitting in a church chair, you need to be paying for that chair. It costs your church money to keep the lights on, the air conditioning on, and the pastor's family fed. If you get something from the pastor's sermons, you need to be giving in the offering. After you have paid your tithes at your local house of God, then you can choose where to start sowing seed.

**170. Bring the whole tithe into the storehouse, not just a part of it.**

The tithe belongs to God. If you give God almost all His money back but keep the rest for yourself, you are a robber. If I found a lost wallet laying on the ground and took a couple of ten dollar bills out of the wallet before returning it to the owner, I would be a thief even though I would have returned most of what he lost. You cannot eat a $5.00 meal deal at McDonalds and walk out after paying $3.00. Pay the whole tithe!

**171. God can do far more with your 90% than you can with 100%.**

A little bit goes a long way when God's blessing is on it.

**172. Tithing honors God.**

Kenneth Copeland said, "Tithing is a matter of honor to me."

Tithing is how you honor God; you acknowledge God's first-place position in your life.

**173. God uses the tithe to test us, and we use the tithe to test God.**

Have you ever wanted to give God a test? God actually challenges us to test Him. If you want to test God, I encourage you to pay your tithe faithfully for one month and see if God brings any blessings your way.

Some people say that we should not test God. They say that testing God is like putting Him in a box. When we say, "God, I'm going to give and that forces You to bless me," that puts God in a box He cannot escape from. It is absolutely right that we should not put God in a box, but in this case, God has put Himself in a box. If God says, "Test Me," I think it is alright to go ahead and test Him. In fact, if we do not test Him in this, we are disobedient.

**174. Tithing disrupts the devil's plans for your life.**

*" 'I will prevent pests from devouring your crops, and the vines in your fields will not cast their fruit," says the LORD Almighty"* (Malachi 3:11).

The King James Version says, "*I will rebuke the devourer for your sakes*" (Malachi 3:11). Who is the devourer? *"Your enemy the devil prowls around like a roaring lion looking for someone to devour"* (1 Peter 5:8). Faithful tithing will ensure that God will rebuke the devil on your behalf.

God's hand of blessing will protect you and your family from the great thief. God will protect you and your business. When the stock market falls or there is a bad economy, God will provide for you in spite of the world's problems.

**175. Tithing releases unprecedented blessing.**

*" 'Then all the nations will call you blessed, for yours will be a delightful land,' says the LORD Almighty"* (Malachi 3:12).

Everyone will recognize how blessed you are. Your house will be blessed. Your business will be blessed. Your family will be blessed! You will have a delightful life!

How can the nations see how blessed you are unless you get

involved in missions? God blesses us so that we can be a blessing to others.

**176. It may appear the wicked suffer no consequences for their failure to give to God, but just wait a little and the difference between the righteous and the unrighteous will be obvious.**

*"'You have said harsh things against Me," says the LORD. 'Yet you ask, "What have we said against You?" You have said, "It is futile to serve God. What did we gain by carrying out His requirements and going about like mourners before the LORD Almighty? But now we call the arrogant blessed. Certainly the evildoers prosper, and even those who challenge God escape." Then those who feared the LORD talked with each other, and the LORD listened and heard. A scroll of remembrance was written in His presence concerning those who feared the LORD and honored His Name. 'They will be Mine,' says the LORD Almighty, 'in the day when I make up my treasured possession. I will spare them, just as in compassion a man spares his son who serves him. And you will again see the distinction between the righteous and the wicked, between those who serve God and those who do not'"* (Malachi 3:13-18). The people were basically saying that there is no difference between the way God treats the wicked and the righteous. God tells them to just wait a little bit in order to see a huge difference in the end results.

**177. Failure to tithe silences God's voice.**

In the last chapter of Malachi, God instructs His people to pay their tithes. Did God's people obey? There must have been a few who obeyed, but the majority of the people continued to rob God. How do I know this? Because God shut up the windows of heaven over Israel. For four hundred years, from Malachi to Matthew, God rarely spoke to His People. The Jews were cut off from God's wisdom for four centuries, partially because they failed to pay their tithes. God gave them a last chance and they failed.

# Secrets of the Seed From Matthew

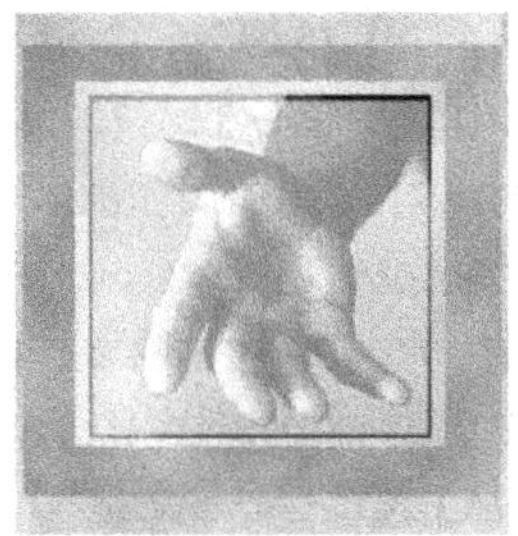

**178. Unforgiveness renders your gifts useless.**

*"Therefore, if you are offering your gift at the altar and there remember that your brother has something against you, leave your gift there in front of the altar. First go and be reconciled to your brother; then come and offer your gift"* (Matthew 5:23-24).

**179. God is an equal opportunity grower.**

The principles of seedtime and harvest work equally for everyone. Jesus explained that God *"causes His sun to rise on the evil and the good, and sends rain on the righteous and the unrighteous"* (Matthew 5:45). God's sun shines upon every field and whatever seeds have been planted begin to grow. God sends rain (equal opportunity) to everyone but the harvest is determined by the seed planted.

**180. Give Secretly**

*"Be careful not to do your 'acts of righteousness' before men, to be seen by them..."* (Matthew 6:1). The Greek verb *theaomai*

translated here "to be seen" gives us our word "theater." The word "hypocrite" means "an actor." If we make a big show of our giving in front of others, we become hypocrites and lose our reward in heaven.

**181. Do not give to impress men, give to impress God.**

*"Be careful not to do your 'acts of righteousness' before men, to be seen by them. If you do, you will have no reward from your Father in heaven. So when you give to the needy, do not announce it with trumpets, as the hypocrites do in the synagogues and on the streets, to be honored by men. I tell you the truth, they have received their reward in full. But when you give to the needy, do not let your left hand know what your right hand is doing, so that your giving may be in secret. Then your Father, who sees what is done in secret, will reward you"* (Matthew 6:1-4).

What are your motives for giving? Are you really interested in helping people or are you just interested in being seen helping people? Do you want men to determine your harvest or God to calculate your harvest? Your harvest can come from men or from God, it is your choice. If you give in secret, God will reward you openly.

**182. You cannot take your money with you to heaven, but you can send it on ahead.**

*"But store up for yourselves treasures in heaven, where moth and rust do not destroy, and where thieves do not break in and steal. For where your treasure is, there your heart will be also"* (Matthew 6:20-21). All that is not given will be lost, but all that you give will be credited to your account forever. We should exchange our earthly treasure for heavenly treasure. Your belongings are not very safe here on earth anyway. Earthly wealth will never last, heavenly wealth will never fade.

There is a legend in church history about Saint Thomas, the same Thomas who doubted Christ's resurrection. While he was in Caesarea, the Lord appeared to him and said, "The king of India, Gondoforus, is seeking workmen to build him a palace finer than the palace of the Emperor of Rome. Behold, I am sending you to him."

Obediently, Thomas went and Gondoforus commanded him to build a magnificent palace and gave him a great quantity of gold and silver to pay for the project. The king left to visit a foreign country and was gone for two years. Meanwhile, Thomas, instead of using the money to build the palace, gave it away to all the poor and sick people in the kingdom. When the king returned, he was angry and he threw Thomas into prison and promised to torture him to death.

But one night the king had a dream of heaven. Angels showed him a wonderful palace made of gold, silver, and numerous precious stones and told him, "This is the palace that Thomas has been building for you." Immediately the king released Thomas from prison. Thomas explained, "Do you not know that those who possess heavenly treasure have little care for the things of this earth? In heaven there are rich palaces prepared for those who purchase them through faith and charity. Your riches, O king, can prepare your way to such a place, but they cannot follow you there."

There is a joke about a man who asked God for special permission to bring one suitcase full of stuff to heaven. He sold everything he owned and filled that suitcase with gold bricks. When he arrived at the pearly gates, the angels looked inside the suitcase and were confused. They asked him, "Why did you bring pavement to heaven?"

When you arrive in heaven, the questions God will ask will not be "How much have you got?" but "How much have you given?" Not, "How much have you won?" but "How much have you done?" Not, "How much have you saved?" but "How many have you saved?" All that matters is what you do with what you have while you are here on earth.

Philanthropists say, "Do your giving while you're living so you'll be knowing where it is going." Pastors say, "Do your sowing before you're going so you'll be knowing where it is growing." If you wait until after you die to give your money away, you run the risk of losing your money to lawyers, estate taxes, relatives, and probate court. Besides, how can God give you a harvest in this life on your seed if you have already crossed over into the afterlife?

There are a variety of trusts and charitable gift annuities which give you assured income for life and the satisfaction of furthering the work of the Lord while saving you thousands of dollars in taxes. Using these tools is like having your cake and eating it too. You can guarantee your income and give to a ministry at the same time. Ask your financial advisor about ways to give your money to a ministry while you are still alive. A wise man once said, "What you save, you leave behind; what you spend, you have for a little while; but what you give away, you take with you."

**183. Your checkbook reveals the condition of your heart.**

*"For where your treasure is, there your heart will be also"* (Matthew 6:21).

**184. Your life can be a manifestation of heaven on earth.**

The Lord's Prayer teaches us to pray, *"Your will be done on earth as it is in heaven"* (Matthew 6:10). What is God's will in heaven? Is there any poverty in heaven? Is there any lack in heaven? Does anyone go hungry in heaven? Do angels get thrown out of mansions because they cannot pay the mortgage in heaven? God wants His will for abundance implemented here on earth the same as it is manifested in heaven. If God's people do not lack in heaven, then God's people should not lack on earth either.

**185. Money can be your lord or money can be your servant.**

If you make Jesus your Lord, then money becomes your servant and you tell it what to do. *"No one can serve two masters. Either he will hate the one and love the other, or he will be devoted to the one and despise the other. <u>You cannot serve both God and Money</u>"* (Matthew 6:24).

**186. Put God first, and you will never lack what you need to eat, drink, and wear.**

Jesus said, *"But seek first His kingdom and His righteousness, and all these things will be given to you as well"* (Matthew 6:33).

**187. God always gives good gifts.**

Jesus said, *"If you, then, though you are evil, know how to give good gifts to your children, how much more will your Father in heaven give good gifts to those who ask Him!"* (Matthew 7:11).

**188. We are blessed so we can be a blessing.**

*"Freely you have received, freely give"* (Matthew 10:8).

**189. If you face a mountain of problems, plant a seed of faith, and your problems will be removed.**

Jesus said, *"If you have faith as small as a mustard seed, you can say to this mountain, 'Move from here to there' and it will move. Nothing will be impossible for you"* (Matthew 17:20). At times everyone faces problems which appear to be as insurmountable as a mountain.

If you plant a seed of faith (even if it is as small as a mustard seed) a miracle will overcome your problems.

**190. You cannot reap where you have not sowed.**

In the parable of the talents, the unfaithful servant accuses his master of *"harvesting where [he had] not sown and gathering where [he had] not scattered seed"* (Matthew 25:24). This statement is false because the master never expected to harvest where he had not sown. He planted five talents into the life of the first servant, two talents into the life of the second servant, and he gave the unfaithful servant one talent. The master simply expected a return on his investment. The first and second servants were rewarded for doubling the master's seed, but the third servant was punished because by misusing his master's seed-money, he had stolen his master's harvest.

**191. If you keep your seed in your hand, what you have right now is the <u>most</u> you will ever have in your lifetime, but if you plant your seed, today's net worth is the <u>least</u> it will ever be.**

Businessmen know that it takes money to make money. In the spiritual realm, it takes seed to produce a harvest. The good news is that God has "given seed to the sower." That means you have seed in your hand right now.

When entrepreneurs decide to start a new business, they look for an "investment angel." This is a bank, investment firm, or rich person who loans them the seed money to start a new corporation. After the new company succeeds, the investor will be richly rewarded. God is your "investment angel." He has given you everything you need to be a success in life.

But as we know from the parable of the talents, it takes more than just having money to make money. You have to do something with the money. The master punished the servant who simply buried his talent. The master asked, "Why didn't you at least put the money in the bank where it would draw interest?"

This same principle is true in the spiritual realm. If you do not use your seed to produce a harvest for the master, your seed will be taken from you and given to someone who is willing to produce a harvest. Don't keep your seed in storage. It is never going to grow if you leave it in your barn.

If you do not plant your seed, the amount of seed you have today is the greatest amount you will ever have for the rest of your life. If your seed is hoarded, it will continually diminish until you are left with nothing. But if you plant your seed, the amount of seed you have in your hands right now is the least amount you will have in your life. Your job is to produce a harvest for your "investment angel." You want to give God a good return on His investment into your life.

Unfortunately, far too many people have defaulted on God's loan. God has given them air to breathe, a planet to live on, talents and abilities to accomplish great things, and seed to sow. But lots of people have eaten their seed, wasted their talents, and squandered the precious time God has given them.

This brings us to an important question for you to ask yourself: Is God's investment in your life producing a return or losing value? If you are not producing harvests, then you are wasting the seed God has placed in your hands.

**192. We should not neglect the tithe, but tithing does not take the place of genuine Christian character.**

Jesus said, *"Woe to you, teachers of the law and Pharisees, you hypocrites! You give a tenth of your spices, mint, dill and cummin. But you have neglected the more important matters of the law, justice, mercy and faithfulness. You should have practiced the latter, without neglecting the former"* (Matthew 23:23).

**193. Giving toward soul winning hastens Christ's return.**

*"This gospel of the kingdom will be preached in the whole world as a testimony to all nations, and then the end will come"* (Matthew 24:14). Do you want Jesus to return? The timetable for His return rests in the hands of the church. As soon as we complete the task He gave us, He will come back for us.

**194. Giving to the poor is giving to the Lord.**

Jesus said, *"...whatever you did for one of the least of these brothers of mine, you did for Me"* (Matthew 25:40).

## Evidence that Jesus was NOT Poor

Religious people say, "I don't care about being rich, I just want to be like Jesus." Do you think Jesus is wearing ragged clothes as He sits upon His throne? I think we should be just like Jesus, and Jesus was rich. Religious tradition has said Jesus was poor, but a look at the facts destroys this myth.

* When Jesus was born, his parents went to the Temple to make a sacrifice. According to Leviticus 12:8, the poor were allowed to sacrifice two turtledoves instead of a lamb. Luke 2:24 says that Mary and Joseph offered turtledoves so apparently they had very little money at this time. But, a short time later, God provided for them by sending rich wisemen to give Jesus an offering. The wise men gave Jesus gifts fit for a King; gold, frankincense, and myrrh (Matthew 2:11). By the way, the wise men started traveling with their gifts two years before they arrived to see the baby Jesus. Immediately after they left, Joseph and Mary were forced to flee to Egypt. God provided for the expenses of their trip to be met long before the expenses were even incurred. This means God has provision headed your way before you even know you have a need.
* Joseph was a carpenter by trade which means the family Jesus grew up in was well off (Matthew 13:55). Even though Jesus was born in a stable, Joseph had planned to rent a room which

means he had at least some money.
* Jesus had so much money, He needed a treasurer to take care of it (John 13:29).
* There was enough money for Judas to steal without anyone noticing (John 12:6).
* The ministry of Jesus had enough money to provide for all the disciples (John 4:8).
* Jesus probably had a house (John 1:37-39, Mark 2:15).
* Jesus had to pay taxes. If you do not have income, you do not have to pay taxes (Matthew 17:27).
* Jesus gave regularly to the poor (John 13:29).
* Jesus had ministry partners who supported His ministry (Luke 8:2-3).
* The clothes Jesus was wearing when He was crucified were so nice the soldiers gambled over who would get them (John 19:23-24).
* When Jesus said, *"Foxes have holes and birds of the air have nests, but the Son of Man has no place to lay His head"* (Matthew 8:20), He was talking about His traveling ministry, not about His financial status. He had just been rejected by a village of the Samaritans (Luke 9:51-53), so this verse does not mean Jesus was homeless, it just means that for that one night He had nowhere to stay.
* When Paul says, *"...Though [Jesus] was rich, yet for your sakes He became poor, so that you through His poverty might become rich"* (2 Corinthians 8:9), he was comparing Christ's heavenly position with His earthly life. The richest king in history is poor compared to the treasures of heaven. It is true that on the cross, Jesus took our sin, our poverty, and our sickness upon Himself. In this sense, He became the poorest man in history, so that we could become rich. Jesus was only poor three days, while He was in the tomb.

# Secrets of the Seed From Mark

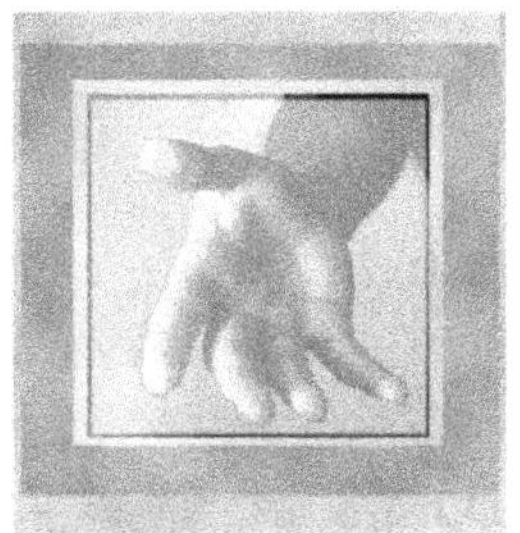

**195. God looks at everything through the paradigm of seed.**

Jesus said, "*A farmer went out to sow his seed...*" (Mark 4:3). This parable demonstrates how God views the world. Later Jesus explains that the seed represents God's Word (Mark 4:14).

**196. Sow your seed, do not just throw your seed.**

"*As he was scattering the seed, some fell along the path...*" (Mark 4:4). If you randomly throw your seed, some of it will land in places that are infertile. In history class as a child, I read about the habits of a tribe of early Native Americans. They carefully dug a hole and dropped three seeds in the hole along with a fish head to fertilize the seeds. This process produced far better results than a haphazard scattering of seed.

**197. Satan will try to eat your harvest.**

"*...and the birds came and ate it up*" (Mark 4:4). The birds in this parable represent Satan (Mark 4:15).

**198. Thousands lose their harvests because of a lack of patience.**

*"Some [seed] fell on rocky places, where it did not have much soil. It sprang up quickly, because the soil was shallow. But when the sun came up, the plants were scorched, and they withered because they had no root"* (Mark 4:5-6).

Many become enthusiastic about sowing for a couple of weeks, but then they stop giving. Later they wonder why they never received a harvest. They complain. They criticize. But the truth is they did not have the patience to outlast "trouble or persecution." Their seed never had the chance to take root. Jesus explained, *"Others, like seed sown on rocky places, hear the word and at once receive it with joy. But since they have no root, they last only a short time. When trouble or persecution comes because of the word, they quickly fall away"* (Mark 4:16-17).

**199. Bad weeds can destroy your good seeds.**

Some *"...seed fell among thorns..."* (Mark 4:7). Thorns are weeds like the worries of this life, the deceitfulness of wealth and the lust for other things (Mark 4:19). Here are some facts about weeds:

1. A weed is any harvest which comes from a bad seed.
2. A weed can choke your seed.
3. In order for your land to produce, you must root up the weeds and plant good seeds.
4. Good seeds and bad weed seeds cannot co-exist. *"Do not plant your field with two kinds of seed"* (Leviticus 19:19).
5. Do not plant bad seed along with your good seed. *"Do not plant two kinds of seed in your vineyard; if you do, not only the crops you plant but also the fruit of the vineyard will be defiled"* (Deuteronomy 22:9).
6. Weed seeds can destroy a field of good seeds.
7. Get the weeds off your seeds. *"See to it that...no bitter root grows up to cause trouble..."* (Hebrews 12:15). Be on guard with your hoe and pull those weeds.
8. What are some weeds that can choke your harvest? *"The worries of this life, the deceitfulness of wealth and the desires for other things..."* (Mark 4:19).

**200. The smart seed-sower knows that good seed can be destroyed by bad soil.**

*"...other seed fell on good soil"* (Mark 4:8). The seed which fell on the path was eaten by birds. The seed which fell among the rocks was scorched by the sun. The seed which fell among the thorns was choked by the weeds. This tells me that not all seed produces a harvest. Why?

There is nothing wrong with your seed. There is nothing wrong with God's principles of sowing and reaping. The problem was in the soil upon which the seed fell. There is some soil unsuitable for your seed. It is vital for you to discern where your seed will produce a good harvest.

Even the seed which fell on the good soil produced a variety of harvests. Some of it reaped a thirty-fold return, some reaped a sixty-fold return, and some reaped a one hundred-fold return. I do not know about you, but I want to believe for the biggest harvest I can possibly get. There is no reason to settle for second best.

Here are some facts about soil:

* The seed cannot change or upgrade the soil.
* Bad soil will destroy good seed.
* Good seed does not change bad soil.
* Don't sow in soil where there is no fruit.
* You must sow into good ground.

**201. Believe God for the hundred-fold return.**

*"...seed fell on good soil. It came up, grew and produced a crop, multiplying thirty, sixty, or even a hundred times"* (Mark 4:8). Seed can produce 30-fold, 60-fold, or 100-fold return. What will your seed produce? Your level of expectation determines your level of manifestation.

**202. With the measure you use, it will be measured back to you.**

Jesus said, *"With the measure you use, it will be measured to you, and even more"* (Mark 4:24). A farmer in Africa asked his neighbors to assist him in harvesting his fields. He asked each of them to bring a basket to help carry the grain. Some of the neighbors brought large baskets, and some used smaller ones. When the work was finished, the farmer measured out their wages by giving each worker ten basketfuls of grain using the same basket they had brought with them. Those with large baskets received large amounts of grain; those working with small baskets received small amounts. The lesson is clear. With the measure you use, it will be measured back to you.

God wants to give you a hundred-fold return on whatever you give. If you measure out your offering in teaspoonfuls, God will give you a harvest of one hundred teaspoonfuls of blessing. If you use a shovel to give, God will multiply back to you one hundred shovelfuls of blessing. If you use a dump truck to haul your gift into church, He will use a dump truck to pour out your blessing.

If you want a harvest in the hundreds of dollars, give in the hundreds. If you want a harvest in the thousands of dollars, give in the thousands. You cannot receive a million-dollar harvest by planting a two-dollar seed. You must gradually increase in order to become a big time harvester.

**203. Sowing seed is a metaphor for the kingdom of God.**

*"This is what the kingdom of God is like. A man scatters seed on the ground. Night and day, whether he sleeps or gets up, the seed sprouts and grows..."* (Mark 4:26-27).

**204. We will never understand how the seed grows.**

*"...the seed sprouts and grows, though he does not know how"* (Mark 4:27). We can observe the results of sowing, but we will never be able to understand exactly how the process works. It is a miracle. This is why people who try to figure out sowing and reaping with their natural minds get confused and begin to criticize what they do not understand.

**205. Once you sow seed, the automatic process of growth kicks in.**

*"All by itself the soil produces grain..."* (Mark 4:28). Once we sow our seed, our involvement is over. God causes it to grow by itself. The seed you put in the ground keeps on growing whether you are sleeping, eating, playing basketball, going to church, or washing your car. You do not even have to pray to make seed grow. Because

of the preprogrammed instructions contained in the DNA of a seed, you cannot stop it from growing once it is in the ground.

**206. Seed growing is a process.**

*"...the soil produces grain first the stalk, then the head, then the full kernel in the head"* (Mark 4:28). For a while you see nothing happening, but underground the little seed is pushing down roots and growing up. One day you see a small sprout appear above the soil. After a while, a stalk grows. Then the head of the grain appears, and finally new seeds are fully formed inside the head of grain. You may just now be seeing the first shoot of your harvest appear.

**207. When harvest time comes, be ready to reap.**

*"As soon as the grain is ripe, he puts the sickle to it..."* (Mark 4:29). Oral Roberts said, "Your miracle is either coming towards you or going past you everyday. If you do not recognize your miracle, you will lose it." When harvest arrives, our sickles must be sharpened and ready to bring in the crop.

**208. Your harvest is coming!**

*"...the harvest has come"* (Mark 4:29). The time will come when the grain is ripe and you will bring in the harvest. The harvest is guaranteed.

**209. Small seeds can produce big harvests.**

Jesus told this parable, *"What shall we say the kingdom of God is like....It is like a mustard seed, which is the smallest seed you plant in the ground. Yet when planted, it grows and becomes the largest of all garden plants, with such big branches that the birds of the air can perch in its shade"* (Mark 4:30-32).

**210. Seed-sowing puts Satan under your feet.**

In Mark 4:4, the birds of the air (which in this parable represent demons) eat the seed. But in Mark 4:32, the mustard seed plant has grown large enough that the birds are under its branches. God will make our harvest so big that the demons that used to eat our seed will be underneath us.

**211. Riches can be deceitful.**

*"Jesus looked around and said to His disciples, 'How hard it is for the rich to enter the kingdom of God!' The disciples were amazed at His words. But Jesus said again, 'Children, how hard it is to enter the kingdom of God! It is easier for a camel to go through the eye of a needle than for a rich man to enter the kingdom of God.'"* (Mark 10:23-25).

You can have money, just do not let money have you. Money is not a measure of true prosperity. Money can buy anything but happiness. It can purchase a ticket to anywhere but heaven. John D. Rockefeller, the richest man of his day, said, "I have made millions but they have brought me no happiness."

Material possessions are not a good measure of prosperity. One person said, "People buy things they don't need, with money they don't have, to impress people they don't like." Those who pursue material possessions end up with maxed-out credit cards and a mailbox full of bills. Besides, the things you own right now, you cannot keep for more than seventy-five or one hundred years. Your house will not last. Soon your car will break down. Your jewelry will be worn by someone else. Everything you own you are leaving right here on earth. I have never seen a hearse pulling a U-Haul, have you?

Here are some thoughts about riches:

* *"...though your riches increase, do not set your heart on them"* (Psalm 62:10).

* *"Whoever trusts in his riches will fall..."* (Proverbs 11:28).

* *"Whoever loves money never has money enough; whoever loves wealth is never satisfied with his income"* (Ecclesiastes 5:10).

* *"There was a man all alone; he had neither son nor brother. There was no end to his toil, yet his eyes were not content with his wealth. 'For whom am I toiling,' he asked, 'and why am I depriving myself of enjoyment?'"* (Ecclesiastes 4:8).

**212. God never forgets a seed sown.**

*"'I tell you the truth,' Jesus replied, 'no one who has left home or brothers or sisters or mother or father or children or fields for Me and the gospel will fail to receive a hundred times as much in this present age (homes, brothers, sisters, mothers, children and*

*fields, and with them, persecutions) and in the age to come, eternal life'"* (Mark 10:29-30).

**213. You can expect a harvest in this life, not just in eternity.**

Some preachers would tell you in this life you can only expect hardship and suffering. They would say your reward will only come after you die. But Jesus says, *"...no one...will fail to receive a hundred times as much in this present age...and in the age to come, eternal life"* (Mark 10:29-30). If you have given up anything for the sake of the gospel, you can rightfully anticipate a hundred-fold harvest.

**214. Even in a time of harvest, Satan will still try to attack you.**

Mark 10:30 points out that even in the midst of receiving a hundred-fold harvest, you will still suffer *"persecutions."* This happens because the devil is jealous of your harvest. He will stir up people against you. But if you will resist the devil, he will flee from you (James 4:7).

**215. Extravagantly giving to Jesus is never a waste.**

Jesus was at a banquet. A woman came with a jar of very expensive perfume worth over $30,000 in today's money. The perfume represented her life's savings. She broke the jar and poured the sweet smelling ointment on Jesus.

Judas was upset. He rebuked her harshly, "Why this waste of perfume? It could have been sold and the money given to the poor."

Jesus said, "Leave her alone. Why are you bothering her? She has done a beautiful thing to Me." When you give a special gift to Jesus, you are doing a beautiful thing.

**216. No matter how much we give to the poor, there will be poor people among us.**

*"The poor you will always have with you..."* (Mark 14:7). Someone once quoted the cliché to Mother Teresa, "Give a man a fish, and he'll be hungry again tomorrow; teach a man to fish, and he'll never be hungry again." She pointed at one of the old, flesh-eaten lepers with whom she worked with and asked, "But what of

those who are unable to fish?" The Christian faith is at its best when we care for the poor, the sick, the hurting, and the helpless.

## Common Excuses for NOT Sowing Seed

I tried it once and nothing happened.
All the preacher wants is my money.
I don't have anything to give.
God doesn't need my money.
Someone else will give.
My spouse doesn't want me to waste our money.
I have too many bills.
I'll give next week.
I need my money for my investments.
When I get rich, then I'll be generous.
I gave last week.
Tithes are only required in the Old Testament.
I can't afford to give.
I'm tired of giving.
I barely have enough to pay my bills.
I am going to save my money for a rainy day,
who knows when I might need it.
I'll catch up on my giving when I get rich.
I'm going through a financial crisis; I can't afford to give.

If you think you can't afford to give, you really can't afford <u>not</u> to give. The worst mistake in the midst of a financial crisis is to quit giving. Let me illustrate. If you need your car to get to work each day, the last thing you do when finances get tight is cut off your car payments. If you lost your car, you could not go to work, you would not make any money, and then you would lose everything. It is the same way with giving. If you stop giving, you lose the vehicle God uses to bless you.

# Secrets of the Seed From Luke

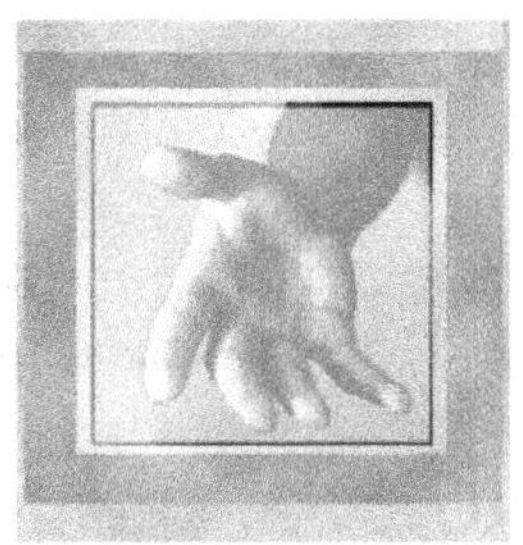

**217. Be poor no more.**

Jesus said, *"The Spirit of the Lord is on Me, because He has anointed Me to preach good news to the poor..."* (Luke 4:18). Jesus was anointed to proclaim good news to poor people. What is good news for the poor? You can be rich, you can prosper, you can live a life of abundance, you don't have to be poor no more.

**218. You can sow your way out of a bad night of fishing.**

Jesus needed a place to stand as He preached. Peter sowed the use of his boat into the life of Jesus. In exchange he received a harvest of a net-breaking, boat-sinking load of fish (Luke 5).

You can sow your way out of a hole. You can sow your way out of debt. You have something you can allow Jesus to use so your harvest can be released.

**219. Sowers sow all the time.**

Jesus said, *"Give to everyone who asks you"* (Luke 6:30). I have never met anyone who fully lives up to this verse.

**220. You can sow once and reap seven times.**

According to Luke 6:38, when you give you will receive seven times.

Give:

1. It will be given to you
2. Good measure
3. Pressed down
4. Shaken together
5. Running over
6. Shall men give into your bosom
7. It will be measured to you.

**221. Giving should happen continuously.**

In Luke 6:38, the Greek word *didote* which is translated "give" is in the continuous present tense. This means we should always be giving. The good news is that when we continuously give, we will also continuously receive.

**222. Giving is the difference between living a useless religion and being a true neighbor.**

Read the story of the Good Samaritan in Luke 10:30-37.

**223. Even if you do not feel worthy to receive, God wants to give to you lavishly.**

In the story of the Prodigal Son (Luke 15:11-32), we see four different mentalities towards God's abundance.

1. The Greedy Mentality - Initially, the younger son was greedy when he asked for his inheritance before the proper time.

2. The Unworthy Mentality - After returning home, the prodigal son felt he was unworthy to receive.

3. The "I Wish I Had a Goat" Mentality - The older brother would have been satisfied with a goat but even though the estate belonged to him he had never even asked for a goat.

4. The Lavish Giving Mentality - The father slaughtered the fatted

calf (his best) in order to celebrate his son's return. If you have an unworthy mentality or a goat mentality, you need to realize that God wants to give you His best.

**224. Lead with your seed.**

*"Whoever can be trusted with very little can also be trusted with much, and whoever is dishonest with very little will also be dishonest with much"* (Luke 16:10).

I was eating lunch with a businessman. I told him about a crusade I was doing where thousands of souls would be saved. I asked him to give a gift to help save their precious lives.

He explained to me that he was working on a multi-million dollar deal. "Soon," he said, "I am going to be very rich. When that happens I plan to give millions of dollars into the kingdom of God." I reiterated that my crusade would take place in just a couple of weeks. I asked him to give a small token gift towards the event. "If you can't give $5,000, then would you give $500, or even $50," I asked.

He refused to give anything. He still has not given anything. His million dollar deal is always just around the corner. Don't wait until you have a million dollars to sow some seed. Start with the $10 you have in your pocket right now. Be faithful with the little you have right now, and God will give you much.

Sowing always precedes reaping. Many get the order backwards. They want to sow after they receive a harvest. They say, "If I make a million dollars, then I will give to God." But God says, "If you want to make a million dollars, then give what you have right now." Give God your "firstfruits" not your "leftovers."

Charles Neiman says, "Promising to give money only if God gives you the money is like a farmer standing in the middle of his field promising to sow seed if he gets a harvest first. Buddy, it ain't gonna happen. A farmer will never reap a harvest before he sows seed. He will only reap after he sows seed."

I used to daydream about what I would give if I suddenly had a million dollars. I planned to give $100,000 to my church and another $100,000 to one of my favorite missionaries and another $100,000 to a television preacher. One day God broke into my daydreaming session and asked me, "What are you going to do with the twenty dollar bill in your pocket?"

I told God, "I am going to use it to buy my lunch today."

God said, "Why don't you give it away?"

"Because I need it in order to pay for lunch," I explained to God.

He replied, "Daniel, if you give the twenty, someday I will trust you to give a million, but if you cannot skip a lunch in obedience to Me, you will never have a million to give."

I gave the money away and fasted lunch that day. I learned that obedience in the small things brings opportunity for big things. The important question for you to ask yourself is not "What would I do if I had a million dollars?" but "What am I doing with the twenty dollars I have in my pocket?"

**225. The Person of Jesus prepares you for eternity. The principles of Jesus prepare you for earth.**

How do I know this? There are people who are good Christians, but are financially poor. When you make Jesus your Lord, His blood cleanses your spirit, but your pocketbook does not change overnight. A change in your economic status requires you to follow Biblical guidelines for wealth creation.

The Bible teaches many principles which lead to wealth. Often the world implements the principles of Jesus better than the church does. For example, in one parable Jesus told of a dishonest manager who acted shrewdly. Jesus pointed out, "*The people of this world are more shrewd in dealing with their own kind than are the people of the light*" (Luke 16:8). We quote the verse often, "The wealth of the wicked is stored up for the righteous," but I think much of the wealth of the wicked can be found in the books which have been published on business principles.

**226. If you are not faithful in paying your tithe, God cannot trust you with deep spiritual insights or supernatural power.**

"*So if you have not been trustworthy in handling worldly wealth, who will trust you with true riches?*" (Luke 16:11).

**227. The refusal to plant a seed guarantees the loss of your harvest.**

One of the greatest harvests ever lost was when Jesus asked the rich young ruler to sell all he had and to give it to the poor (Luke 18:22). The man went away sad because he was very wealthy. Jesus asked him to sow earthly riches in exchange for eternal life and a place on Jesus' staff. He gave up a place in the kingdom and apostleship for the sake of a little money.

Every instruction you receive from God has a reward attached to your obedience. When you obey, you receive your reward. When you disobey, you lose your reward.

**228. It is not the amount you put in the offering that impresses God, it is the amount you have left over afterwards that impresses Him.**

*"As He looked up, Jesus saw the rich putting their gifts into the temple treasury. He also saw a poor widow put in two very small copper coins. 'I tell you the truth,' He said, 'this poor widow has put in more than all the others. All these people gave their gifts out of their wealth; but she out of her poverty put in all she had to live on'"* (Luke 21:1-4). Put this book down and find two pennies to hold in your hand as you read this story.

The disciples were watching the rich people bring bags full of money to the temple. Dressed in their best clothing, these men displayed their wealth for all to see. It impressed the disciples, but it did not impress Jesus.

What moved Jesus? Two small copper coins (the equivalent of two pennies) did not look like a very big offering. But Jesus turned to His disciples and said, "this poor widow has put in more than all the others." Can you imagine? The widow's two coins were worth more than the combined total of every other gift.

Robb Thompson says, "The value of a gift is not in what you give. The value of a gift is in what it cost you to give it."

The widow woman is called "poor." In the original Greek language the word used here is *penichros,* which means "conspicuously needy." But this word also means "hard working." In other words, this woman worked for her daily bread. Money did not come easily to her. She had to work hard for it, save it, and spend it carefully. She had to make every penny count.

The rich people gave out of their abundance, their overflow, their leftovers. But the widow woman gave out of her desperate need. She put God first by putting in her best gift, the result of her hard labor.

You can probably relate to the widow woman. You may not be desperately poor, but I am sure you work hard for your money. I am also sure you have some financial needs right now. You are not where you need to be to fully complete your vision and mission in life.

It is not the size of your offering that matters to God, it is the size of your heart.

**229. The smart seed-sower realizes that every gift is important (no matter the size of the gift).**

Every gift is important. God's master plan of provision for the church includes your gift, no matter how small and insignificant it seems. God does not tell all to give the same amount, but God does tell us all to give the amount we need to give. If each believer would just do his or her part, every need in the body of Christ would be met.

When Nehemiah rebuilt the wall of Jerusalem, each family was assigned a different length of wall. Some families were able to build more than other families, but each part was important. If just one family had failed to complete their task, the entire city would have been vulnerable to enemy attack.

Satan tries to deceive many by telling them their gifts are too small to be worth giving. This is the enemy's way of trying to steal your harvest. A tiny seed planted in obedience is equal in value to the largest amount ever given.

# Secrets of the Seed From John

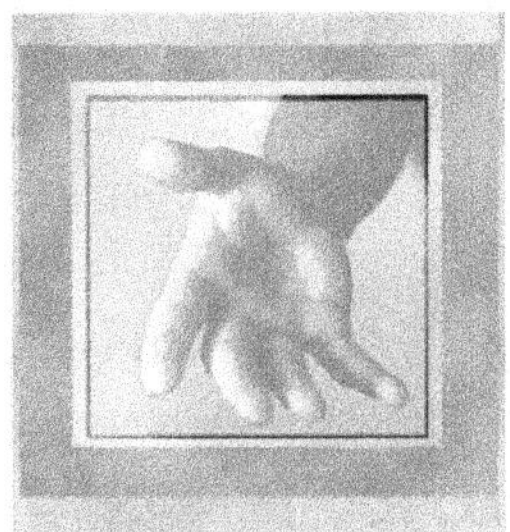

**230. Giving is an expression of love.**

*"For God so loved the world that He gave..."* (John 3:16). Because God loves the world, He gave His only Son. When a boy loves his girlfriend, he gives her roses and chocolates. When a man loves a woman, he gives her a diamond ring as a token of his love. When a mother and father love their daughter, they give her presents on her birthday and at Christmas and at random times in between. Your giving to God is an expression of your love for God. Amy Carmichael said, "You can give without loving, but you cannot love without giving."

**231. Those who give toward preaching the gospel will receive the same reward as those who preach the gospel.**

*"Do you not say, 'Four months more and then the harvest?' I tell you, open your eyes and look at the fields! They are ripe for harvest. Even now the reaper draws his wages, even now he harvests the crop for eternal life, so that the sower and the reaper may be glad*

*together. Thus the saying 'One sows and another reaps' is true. I sent you to reap what you have not worked for. Others have done the hard work, and you have reaped the benefits of their labor"* (John 4:35-38).

In this passage Jesus is talking about the harvest fields of world evangelism. In Matthew 9:37 Jesus said to His disciples, *"The harvest is plentiful but the workers are few."* There are millions of souls who are ready to be saved, if only someone would tell them the good news.

One person sows, another reaps, but both rejoice together. As an evangelist, I often reap souls. In one of my recent crusades, over ten thousand people were saved in one night. However, even though I had the pleasure of leading sinners in a prayer of salvation, behind me stood many ministry partners who gave me money to make that event possible. Each of them share in the harvest.

Ministers who reap a harvest of souls and the sowers who planted seed to make the harvest possible will share the rewards of evangelism. *"The share of the man who stayed with the supplies is to be the same as that of him who went down to the battle. All will share alike"* (1 Samuel 30:24).

**232. Jesus came to give you a life of abundance.**

*"The thief cometh not, but for to steal, and to kill, and to destroy: I am come that they might have life, and that they might have it more abundantly"* (John 10:10 KJV). Poverty is caused by that thieving, lying, good-for-nothing, cattle-rustler named Lucifer. Jesus came to give us an abundant life including abundant finances, abundant health, and abundant blessings.

**233. Sowing is one of the greatest weapons in the arsenal of spiritual warfare.**

You don't need to take back what the devil stole; you don't want that old junk anyway. What you need to do is sow your way to a harvest. Don't react to the devil; let the devil react to you.

**234. Jesus was the greatest Seed ever sown, and He produced the greatest harvest ever reaped.**

The saddest day in heaven was when Adam and Eve were

separated from God by their sin. Immediately God responded by promising a seed which would correct the problem. He knew that only the power of a seed was greater than the power of sin. He said to the serpent, "The Seed of the woman shall bruise your head."

Thousands of years later this prophecy was fulfilled. The Holy Spirit came upon the virgin Mary and planted a God-seed within her womb. This Seed was Jesus Christ.

Jesus is called:

- the Seed of the woman (Genesis 3:15)
- the Seed of Abraham (Galatians 3:29)
- the Seed of David (Romans 1:3)
- the incorruptible Seed (1 Peter 1:23)

God literally planted Himself. Only a seed of infinite magnitude would produce a harvest which could defeat sin. God gave Jesus so that He could have you.

A seed must die before it will produce a harvest (John 12:24). Jesus knew that in order to produce a harvest of forgiveness, He would have to die.

The God-seed died on the cross to pay the price for our sins. Jesus gave His life so He could save your life. A seed must leave the hand of the sower and enter the ground and die before it can produce a harvest. Jesus was separated from God, He died, and was placed in the ground for three days. But on the third day, the harvest began!

The Father planted one Son and reaped millions of sons and daughters. God gave His best so that He could have a family. This was the greatest harvest in history and it is not done yet. God is still reaping souls every day.

If Satan had understood the concept of seed-power, he never would have killed Jesus. The ironic fact is that the devil had thousands of years to observe the way seeds work to produce harvests. He failed to recognize that the natural process of sowing and reaping is a reflection of a spiritual process which is the key to the greatest power in the universe.

God's kingdom functions on the principles of giving. Satan's kingdom was founded on the principles of taking. Satan cannot understand why the more he takes the less he has, and why the more God gives the more God has.

**235. The smart seed-sower recognizes that a seed in hand will never produce a harvest until it is planted.**

*"I tell you the truth, unless a kernel of wheat falls to the ground and dies, it remains only a single seed. But if it dies, it produces many seeds"* (John 12:24). John Avanzini says, "You must render your seed useless." The seed must leave your hand, it must enter the ground, it must be rendered useless, it must die; then and only then can it produce a harvest.

One day God asked me, "How much does a seed in your hand produce?" I realized that a seed in my hand will never grow until I sow it. My seed has no harvest potential until I plant it. If you keep what you presently have, that is the most it will ever be. When you sow it, that is the least it will ever be.

**Picture your harvest as you plant your seed**

My sister Melody loves to garden. In the spring she buys little packets of seeds from the nursery. On the front of each package is a picture of the harvest. As my sister sows her garden, she has a mental picture of what it is going to look like. She plans for one type of flower to blossom here and another plant to grow there. We should do the same as we plant our seeds. We should have a vision of what our harvest is going to look like.

# Secrets of the Seed From Acts

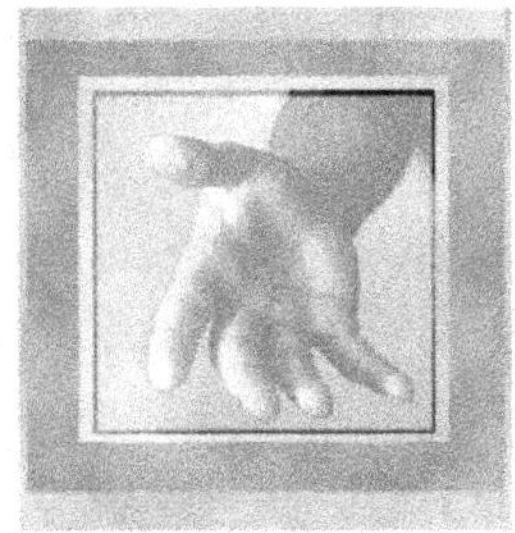

**236. If every believer would give, there would be no needy in the church.**

*"Neither was there any among them that lacked: for as many as were possessors of lands or houses sold them, and brought the prices of the things that were sold, And laid them down at the apostles' feet: and distribution was made unto every man according as he had need"* (Acts 4:34-35 KJV).

**237. Your giving encourages the church.**

*"...Barnabas...of the country of Cyprus, having land, sold it, and brought the money, and laid it at the apostles' feet"* (Acts 4:36-37 KJV). Barnabas (his name means Son of Encouragement) was from Cyprus which was a tourist destination in the Roman world. Land in Cyprus was very expensive. When he sold his property and gave the money from the sale to the apostles, the large sum really blessed the early church.

**238. Do not give because people are watching, give because God is watching.**

Ananias and Sapphira were probably jealous because before Barnabas' gift they might have been the biggest givers in the church. The attention of the people left them and centered upon Barnabas. In order to recapture attention, they sold their biggest plot of land. But they did not want to actually give that much money to the apostles, they only wanted to appear to have given all the money from the land to the apostles. So they lied and died because they tried to fool God (Acts 5:1-11).

**239. Our prayers and our giving work together to attract the attention of God.**

There was a Roman centurion named Cornelius. *"He and all his family were devout and God-fearing; he gave generously to those in need and prayed to God regularly"* (Acts 10:2). Even though Cornelius was a Gentile, God took notice of him. Prior to this the Jews were God's chosen people and were blessed because of their relationship with God. However, Cornelius' habit of giving caught God's attention. One day an angel appeared to him and said, *"Your prayers and gifts to the poor have come up as a memorial offering before God"* (Acts 10:4). Because of this vision, Cornelius became the first Gentile to be saved. His giving released the harvest of salvation for all Gentiles.

**240. Giving is better than receiving.**

*"...the Lord Jesus Himself said: 'It is more blessed to give than to receive"* (Acts 20:35). Giving is better than receiving, but I enjoy both sides of the equation. However, the joy of receiving only lasts until the object wears out or becomes boring, but the joy of giving lasts for an eternity. I remember the gifts I give far longer than I remember the gifts people give me.

# Secrets of the Seed From Romans

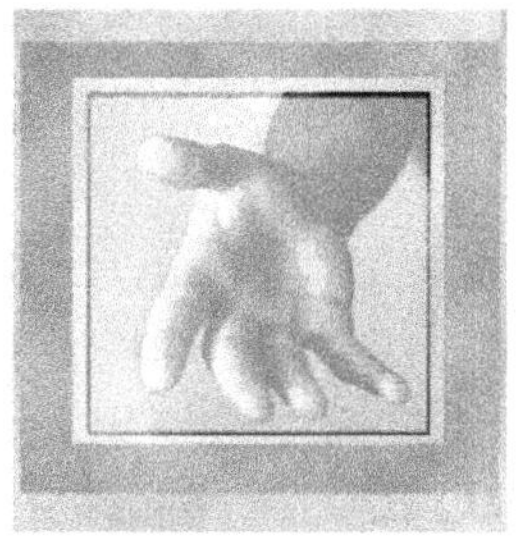

**241. You can live a life of victory.**

*"...We are more than conquerors through Him who loved us"* (Romans 8:37). If you are living a defeated, poverty-stricken life, you are less than a conqueror. A conqueror rules over everything in sight. Imagine what it is like to be more than a conqueror.

**242. Your money makes a difference in eternity.**

*'"Everyone who calls on the name of the Lord will be saved.' How, then, can they call on the One they have not believed in? And how can they believe in the One of whom they have not heard? And how can they hear without someone preaching to them? And how can they preach unless they are sent?"* (Romans 10:13-15). In order for today's preacher to be sent, someone must give money to help buy the plane ticket. Money is needed to pay for sound systems, television time, literature distribution, etc.

**243. Giving is a spiritual gift.**

*"We have different gifts, according to the grace given us. If a man's gift is prophesying, let him use it in proportion to his faith. If it is serving, let him serve; if it is teaching, let him teach; if it is encouraging, let him encourage; if it is contributing to the needs of others, let him give generously; if it is leadership, let him govern diligently; if it is showing mercy, let him do it cheerfully"* (Romans 12:6-8).

One of my giftings is to preach, but when I first started preaching I was not a good preacher. I developed my gift and as I worked at it, that anointing become more evident in my life.

You can develop the gift of giving in your life. You may have a special anointing for giving upon your life that you have not discovered yet. Until you start practicing the art of giving, you will never know.

Your life of giving can begin now. Theodore Roosevelt said, "Do what you can, with what you have, where you are." Plant whatever seed you have right where you are.

**244. Preachers deserve to be blessed for their labor.**

Paul explained, *"...when the plowman plows and the thresher threshes, they ought to do so in the hope of sharing in the harvest. If we have sown spiritual seed among you, is it too much if we reap a material harvest from you? If others have this right of support from you, shouldn't we have it all the more? ...Don't you know that those who work in the temple get their food from the temple, and those who serve at the altar share in what is offered on the altar? In the same way, the Lord has commanded that those who preach the gospel should receive their living from the gospel"* (1 Corinthians 9:10-14).

**Reasons to give generously to your man of God**

* If you keep your preacher poor he will never be able to lead you to wealth.
* Jesus said *"The worker deserves his wages"* (Luke 10:7) and Paul repeated it (1 Timothy 5:18).
* When a mechanic repairs your car, he sets the price. When you order food in a restaurant, the menu tells you what to pay. Yet ministers

allow you to give what you feel like giving. Even if you refuse to give in the offering, they still preach you a sermon. No one would criticize a restaurant by saying, "All they want is your money" yet people say this about preachers every day. On average, preachers are paid less for more hours of labor than hundreds of other professions.

* Entertainment at a movie costs $5-$10 for each ticket. Professional counseling could cost $100 an hour. Childcare for two hours might cost $15. Healing through modern medicine costs thousands of dollars. Motivational speakers charge hundreds of dollars for their sessions. Churches offer these benefits at a small fraction of the cost. We should do what we can to support those who are there to help us when we are in need.

* Paul said, *"The elders who direct the affairs of the church well are worthy of double honor, especially those whose work is preaching and teaching"* (1 Timothy 5:17). The Greek word *time* (pronounced tee-may) which this verse translates as "honor" also carries the meaning of "honorarium" or "compensation." So, we should honor our preachers by rewarding them generously for their work.

* Twice Paul quotes the Old Testament saying, *"Do not muzzle an ox while it is treading out the grain"* (1 Corinthians 9:9; 1 Timothy 5:18). While an ox is working, it is wrong to prevent it from enjoying the fruits of its labor. This same principle applies to pastors.

**245. It is the responsibility of ministers to never allow the pursuit of money to hinder the preaching of the gospel.**

Paul, after building his case concerning the rights of preachers to receive money, explained, *"...we did not use this right. On the contrary, we put up with anything rather than hinder the gospel of Christ"* then he says it again, *"But I have not used any of these rights. And I am not writing this in the hope that you will do such things for me. I would rather die than have anyone deprive me of this boast. Yet when I preach the gospel, I cannot boast, for I am compelled to preach. Woe to me if I do not preach the gospel!"* (1 Corinthians 9:12,15-16).

God has placed a solemn responsibility in the hands of His ministers. When preachers mishandle finances, become greedy, or focus so much on money that they cease helping people, they betray

God's trust. God wants His servants to be blessed, but souls are His first priority.

**246. Give Systematically.**

*"On the first day of every week, each one of you should set aside a sum of money in keeping with his income, saving it up, so that when I come no collections will have to be made"* (1 Corinthians 16:2).

Giving should become a discipline. The lottery is a fantasy yet people will spend money every week trying to win against tremendous odds. The same people will tithe one Sunday and complain that nothing happened. That is like a farmer planting only a few rows of corn and complaining that the rest of the field is empty at harvest time. To produce the best results, giving must be systematically implemented over a period of time. The lottery is a fantasy. Credit card debt is foolish. Tithing is a command. Giving is a discipline.

**Give your seed an assignment**

Target your seed. Be precise in your request. What do you want God to do? Be clear. Never put money in an offering without giving it an assignment. This is the only way you know whether your seed is working or not. If you are too general in your request, you will never know if your giving is producing results or not. Mike Murdock says, "If you just tell God that you want to be richer, the next time you find a nickel, your wish comes true." Tell your money to go and grow. Look at your bill as you put it in the offering and say, "Bring back your big friends."

# Secrets of the Seed
# Jerusalem Offering

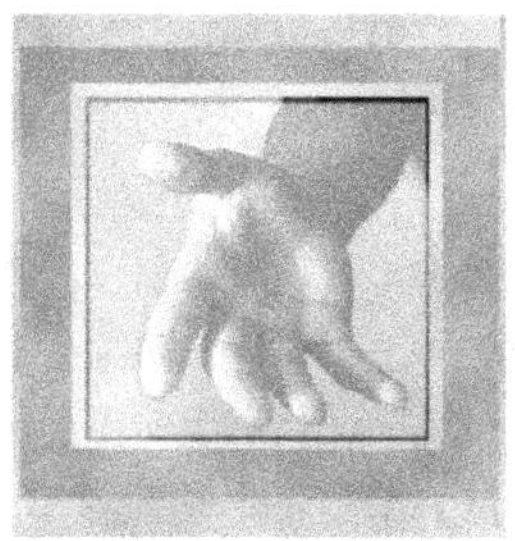

The Apostle Paul was deeply committed to giving. His giving nature is revealed by his dedication to helping the church in Jerusalem when they were in need (2 Corinthians 8-9). In Acts 11:27-29, the prophet Agabus prophesied that a severe famine would spread over the entire Roman world. The prophecy came true and the Jewish historian Josephus describes how the famine devastated the land of the Jews (Antiquities XX). The severeness of this famine is attested to by several Roman historians including Suetonius, Tacitus, and Dio Cassius. Many Jews died from starvation, and the Jerusalem church was hit particularly hard.

In the midst of the hardship, Paul came to the rescue! The church in Antioch took up an offering to help the church in Jerusalem and they entrusted it to Paul and Barnabas. When Paul arrived in Jerusalem, he witnessed the value of the gift he brought. Throughout the rest of his missionary career, Paul had a soft spot in his heart for the needs of the Jerusalem church and he repeatedly asked churches to take up an offering for the mother church. Peter, James, and John specifically asked him to remember the poor of Jerusalem, and Paul replied that he was already eager to do so (Galatians 2:10).

Paul did remember the church in Jerusalem. Toward the end of his third missionary journey, Paul received word that the Jerusalem church was struggling again. He decided to bless them by taking up an offering among the Gentile churches he had planted in Macedonia and Achaia including the churches of Corinth, Athens, Berea, Thessalonica, and Philippi.

Paul instructed the churches to set aside money each Sunday for the saints in Jerusalem (1 Corinthians 16:1-4). Even though the churches of Macedonia were in extreme poverty (2 Corinthians 8:2), they gave with overflowing joy and with rich generosity. Paul uses their example to encourage the Corinthians to give equally generously (2 Corinthians 9:4-5). Over a period of time, a substantial sum was gathered and Paul and a group of men took it to Jerusalem, despite the danger this entailed for Paul's life (Romans 15:31).

Paul's gift to the church in Jerusalem opened the door for the Gentiles to be set free from living under the oppressive law. When Paul and Barnabas took the first offering to Jerusalem, a portion of the church was trying to impose certain Jewish customs upon Gentile converts (Galatians 2). Paul's words, combined with the seed planted by Gentiles, convinced Peter, James, and John to allow Gentiles to live in freedom instead of under the law.

Paul points out that since the Jews have blessed us, we should bless them in return (Romans 15:27). The Gentile Christians are encouraged to give to the Jewish Christians because they have shared in the Jewish spiritual blessing. The Gentiles owe a debt of gratitude to the Jews.

The offering for the church in Jerusalem is the context for the two greatest giving chapters in the Bible, 2 Corinthians 8-9. This passage is where we get many treasured promises concerning giving.

**247. Give, even in the midst of difficult economic times.**

*"And now, brothers, we want you to know about the grace that God has given the Macedonian churches. Out of the most severe trial, their overflowing joy and their extreme poverty welled up in rich generosity. For I testify that they gave as much as they were able, and*

*even beyond their ability. Entirely on their own, they urgently pleaded with us for the privilege of sharing in this service to the saints. And they did not do as we expected, but they gave themselves first to the Lord and then to us in keeping with God's will. So we urged Titus, since he had earlier made a beginning, to bring also to completion this act of grace on your part"* (2 Corinthians 8:1-6).

**248. God is more interested in us than in our money.**

*"...they gave themselves first to the Lord"* (2 Corinthians 8:5). Unless we give ourselves to the Lord first, our money gifts will be pointless.

**249. Your giving can serve as an example for others.**

Paul used the example of the Corinthian church's vow to give to motivate the Macedonian church to give. In this letter, he encourages the Corinthian church to complete their vow by emphasizing how much the Macedonian church gave even when they were in great need.

**250. We should excel in the grace of giving.**

*"But just as you excel in everything, in faith, in speech, in knowledge, in complete earnestness and in your love for us, see that you also excel in this grace of giving"* (2 Corinthians 8:7).

**251. Giving is not a command, it is a test.**

*"I am not commanding you, but I want to test the sincerity of your love by comparing it with the earnestness of others"* (2 Corinthians 8:8).

**252. If Jesus was willing to give up the luxuries of heaven for our sake, we should be willing to give up everything for His sake.**

*"For you know the grace of our Lord Jesus Christ, that though He was rich, yet for your sakes He became poor, so that you through His poverty might become rich"* (2 Corinthians 8:9).

**253. Always pay your vows.**

*"And here is my advice about what is best for you in this mat-*

*ter: Last year you were the first not only to give but also to have the desire to do so. Now finish the work, so that your eager willingness to do it may be matched by your completion of it, according to your means"* (2 Corinthians 8:10-11). We must finish what we start. Robb Thompson says, "We are only rewarded for our actions, never for our intentions." If you have ever made a vow to the Lord and failed to complete it, God's hand of blessing is stopped until you keep your word.

**254. God wants us to be willing to give.**

*"For if the willingness is there..."* (2 Corinthians 8:12).

**255. God asks us to give what we have, not what we do not have.**

*"...the gift is acceptable according to what one has, not according to what he does not have"* (2 Corinthians 8:12).

**256. It is not right for us to live in abundance when our brothers live in poverty.**

*"Our desire is not that others might be relieved while you are hard pressed, but that there might be equality"* (2 Corinthians 8:13).

**257. What you sow, comes back to you.**

*"At the present time your plenty will supply what they need, so that in turn their plenty will supply what you need. Then there will be equality, as it is written: 'He who gathered much did not have too much, and he who gathered little did not have too little'"* (2 Corinthians 8:14-15). When you give to others when they are in need, God will make sure others will give to you when you are in need.

**258. Your giving is noticed.**

*"I thank God, who put into the heart of Titus the same concern I have for you. For Titus not only welcomed our appeal, but he is coming to you with much enthusiasm and on his own initiative. And we are sending along with him the brother who is praised by all the churches for his service to the gospel. What is more, he was chosen by the churches to accompany us as we carry the offering, which we administer in order to honor the Lord Himself and to show our ea-*

*gerness to help....In addition, we are sending with them our brother who has often proved to us in many ways that he is zealous, and now even more so because of his great confidence in you. As for Titus, he is my partner and fellow worker among you; as for our brothers, they are representatives of the churches and an honor to Christ. Therefore show these men the proof of your love and the reason for our pride in you, so that the churches can see it"* (2 Corinthians 8:16-24).

**259. Giving is the only way to prove your love.**

*"...show these men the proof of your love..."* (2 Corinthians 8:24). A man proves his love for his wife when he sacrificially gives to her by taking out the trash when he could be watching the big game. A mother proves her love for her children when she gives them new clothes for school. We prove our love for God when we give in church. There are many who say they love, but there are few who prove it.

**260. Ministers must be above reproach when handling money.**

*"We want to avoid any criticism of the way we administer this liberal gift. For we are taking pains to do what is right, not only in the eyes of the Lord but also in the eyes of men"* (2 Corinthians 8:20-21).

**261. Our enthusiasm about giving motivates others to give.**

*"There is no need for me to write to you about this service to the saints. For I know your eagerness to help, and I have been boasting about it to the Macedonians, telling them that since last year you in Achaia were ready to give; and your enthusiasm has stirred most of them to action"* (2 Corinthians 9:1-2).

**262. Take time to prepare your seed before you sow it.**

*"But I am sending the brothers in order that our boasting about you in this matter should not prove hollow, but that you may be ready, as I said you would be. For if any Macedonians come with me and find you unprepared, we, not to say anything about you, would be ashamed of having been so confident. So I thought it necessary to urge the brothers to visit you in advance and <u>finish the arrangements</u>*

*for the generous gift you had promised. Then it will be ready as a generous gift, not as one grudgingly given"* (2 Corinthians 9:3-5).

**263. If you sow a lot, you reap a lot; if you sow a little, you reap a little.**

*"Remember this: Whoever sows sparingly will also reap sparingly, and whoever sows generously will also reap generously"* (2 Corinthians 9:6).

**264. Do not give just because someone forces you to give.**

*"Each man should give what he has decided in his heart to give, not reluctantly or under compulsion, for God loves a cheerful giver"* (2 Corinthians 9:7).

**265. God loves a cheerful giver**

*"God loves a cheerful giver"* (2 Corinthians 9:7). The word "cheerful" comes from the Greek word *hilaros* which is where we get our word "hilarious." Offering time should be a happy time. Our attitude about giving is just as important as the gift we give.

**266. God's definition of prosperity includes having all you need with enough left over to be a blessing to everyone you come in contact with.**

*"And God is able to make all grace abound to you, so that in all things at all times, having all that you need, you will abound in every good work"* (2 Corinthians 9:8).

**267. God scatters seed among the poor.**

*"He has scattered abroad His gifts to the poor; His righteousness endures forever"* (2 Corinthians 9:9). This is a quote from Psalm 112:9.

**268. The seed we sow comes from God.**

*"Now He who supplies seed to the sower and bread for food will also supply and increase your store of seed and will enlarge the harvest of your righteousness"* (2 Corinthians 9:10).

**269. God gives seed to the sower...not to the one who hoards.**

God gives *"seed to the sower."* Imagine a farmer who is planting crops. He hires laborers to help him sow. As he watches them work, he notices some who are diligent about sowing seed. Then he notices others who sit down under a tree and refuse to work. Who is the farmer going to give more seed too? Those who sow are given more seed; those who refuse to sow will lose what they have.

**270. The purpose of wealth is generosity.**

*"You will be made rich in every way so that you can be generous on every occasion, and through us your generosity will result in thanksgiving to God"* (2 Corinthians 9:11). Andrew Carnegie, who made a fortune selling steel, said, "The sole purpose of being rich is to give away money."

**271. Giving blesses God and blesses God's people.**

*"This service that you perform is not only supplying the needs of God's people but is also overflowing in many expressions of thanks to God. Because of the service by which you have proved yourselves, men will praise God for the obedience that accompanies your confession of the gospel of Christ, and for your generosity in sharing with them and with everyone else"* (2 Corinthians 9:12-13).

**272. It is the responsibility of those who receive to offer prayers on behalf of those who give.**

*"And in their prayers for you their hearts will go out to you, because of the surpassing grace God has given you"* (2 Corinthians 9:14). In my ministry, I pray daily for the people who have partnered with me. Their concerns become my concerns. Their prayer requests become my priority. Why? Because their giving has linked them to my heart.

**273. We give because God gave first.**

*"Thanks be to God for His indescribable gift!"* (2 Corinthians 9:15).

## It's all Greek to Me

In 2 Corinthians chapters 8-9, Paul uses several Greek words to describe the Jerusalem offering. His use of these words reveal what the giving of an offering means to us today. Paul chose his words carefully and each word he uses here is full of deep spiritual meaning.

*Charis:* Paul uses this word ten times in two chapters to refer to the "grace of giving." At a basic level this word means "grace," but it means much more than that. One scholar says it means "divine generosity lavishly bestowed." When God gives us grace, we do not deserve or merit it. It is a free gift which flows from God's great love for us. This grace has been abundantly and liberally poured upon us. In turn we give back to God.

The word *charis* is the root word for the term "Charismatic" which is used to describe Christians who believe in the gifts of the Spirit. But Paul's use of this word to refer to an offering reveals a new meaning to living a charismatic life. Not only should Charismatics rejoice in the gifts of the Spirit to believers, they should also be the most joyful givers in the Church. Just as the Spirit gives gifts, we should give gifts.

*Didomi:* (2 Cor. 8:5) means "to give" or "to bestow a gift."

*Diakonia:* (2 Cor. 8:4; 9:13) This means "ministry" or "service." Giving is a ministry to others, it is an act of service.

*Koinonia:* (2 Cor. 8:4; 9:13) This word means "fellowship." Giving is an act of fellowship and brotherhood. As we give we come closer together, we come into unity. The more you give the more tied in you are to the church family.

*Leitourgia:* (2 Cor. 9:12) This word is where we get our word "liturgy" from. In many churches a specific liturgy guides worshipers in their worship. This word was used to describe the service of the priests in the temple worship. Their job was to worship God all day long, and Paul uses the word to tell us that giving is an act of worship.

Your whole life is an act of worship. Every part of your life must line up with your expression of faith. If you raise your hands and don't give in the offering you have not worshiped. If you sang your very best but fail to give your very best, you are not fully worshiping.

*Doxa:* (2 Cor. 9:13) This word means "glory." Our cheerful and joyful giving glorifies God. *"You will be glorifying God through your generous gifts"* (2 Corinthians 9:13 NLT).

# Secrets of the Seed From Galatians

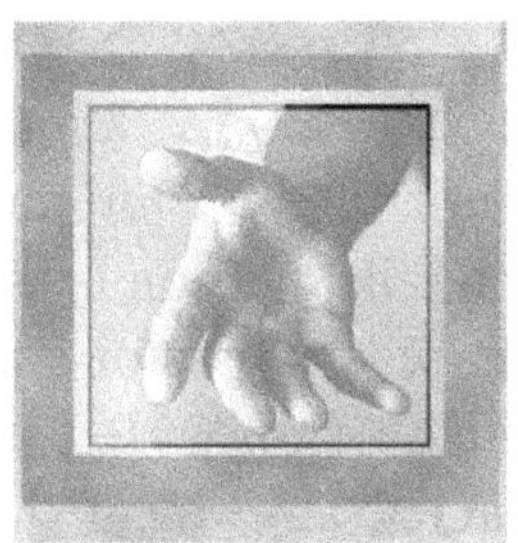

**274. The principle of sowing and reaping is an eternal law of God's creation.**

*"Do not be deceived: God cannot be mocked..."* (Galatians 6:7*)*. Do not fool yourself, you cannot ignore God's laws, whatsoever a man sows, that shall he also reap. If you sow good seeds, you will reap a good harvest. If you sow bad seeds, you will reap a bad harvest.

**275. The smart seed-sower knows that systematic giving produces regular harvests.**

*"...whatsoever a man soweth, that shall he also reap"* (Galatians 6:7 KJV). In the Greek language, the word "soweth" is in the continuous present tense. This means sowing is not a one-time action, instead, it denotes a person who is always sowing. So this verse could be translated "Whatever a man sows, and sows, and sows, and sows, and continues to sow..." The word "reap" is in the same tense which means the second part of this verse could be translated "that shall he also reap, and reap, and reap, and reap, and continue to reap."

**276. If you sow into the distractions of the flesh, you will reap the destruction of the flesh.**

*"The one who sows to please his sinful flesh, from that flesh will reap destruction..."* (Galatians 6:8). If you use your money to buy the gaudy toys of this world which are born of lust, ego, envy, and pride you will eventually earn for yourself eternal destruction in the pit of hell. Sin will take you farther than you want to go, keep you longer than you want to stay, and cost you more than you want to pay.

**277. If you sow in obedience to the voice of the Spirit, you will reap eternal life.**

*"...the one who sows to please the Spirit, from the Spirit will reap eternal life"* (Galatians 6:8). Our number one goal should be to please the Spirit of God. His opinion is the only one that really matters. Do not sow to please your pastor, or your spouse, or your own ego, sow to please the Holy Spirit. He is the only One who can give you a harvest of eternal life anyway.

**278. The smart seed-sower never tires of sowing.**

Paul reminds us, *"Let us not become weary in doing good, for at the proper time we will reap a harvest if we do not give up"* (Galatians 6:9). Weariness is one of the greatest thieves of harvests in the body of Christ. Due to our fleshly nature it is easy to get tired of doing what is right, but the greatest rewards go to those who stick with the race until the end. Exhaustion, fatigue, weariness, wanting to throw in the towel, or giving up destroys thousands of harvests every day. For years people will be faithful to give to God and then, right before their harvest arrives, they give up. They stop hoping for a harvest and the harvest is lost.

The leper Naaman was told by the prophet Elisha to dip in the Jordan River seven times to cure his leprosy (2 Kings 5). The first six times he dipped he could perceive no change in his body, but on the seventh dip he was completely healed. If he had given up on the sixth dip, he would not have received his harvest. Your harvest is right around the corner, do not give up.

**279. The smart seed-sower remembers there are seasons for both sowing and reaping.**

A farmer who looks out his window the morning after sowing is not disappointed when the fields still look bare. He is happy with his sowing because he knows that with the changing of the seasons, his harvest will come. The NIV says *"at the proper time we will reap a harvest."* The KJV says *"in due season we shall reap."* The original Greek word for this "proper time" is *kairos* which means "appointed time, opportune or seasonable time, or the right time." This word refers to the God-ordained and God-controlled moment for your harvest. Here are some facts about your "due season."

* **Everything, including your harvest, has an appointed season.**

*"To every thing there is a season, and a time to every purpose under the heaven"* (Ecclesiastes 3:1 KJV).

* **God controls the seasons.**

*"Then I will give you rain in due season, and the land shall yield her increase, and the trees of the field shall yield their fruit"* (Leviticus 26:4 KJV).

* **Rain shall come in due season and the harvest shall come in due season.**

*"I will give you the rain of your land in his due season, the first rain and the latter rain, that thou mayest gather in thy corn..."* (Deuteronomy 11:14 KJV).

* **Every season has a reason!**

* **We must do our giving in due season, if we want to receive a harvest in due season.**

A farmer who does not plant in the spring will not receive a harvest in the fall. There is a proper season for giving and we must learn to recognize that season if we expect to receive a harvest during its proper season. God said to Moses, *"Command the children of Israel, and say unto them, My offering...shall ye observe to offer unto Me in their due season"* (Numbers 28:2 KJV).

*** We should look to God to give us a harvest in due season.**

*"These all look to You to give them their food [in due season]. When You give it to them, they gather it up; when You open your hand, they are satisfied with good things"* (Psalm 104:27-28). This concept is repeated in Psalm 145:15-16, *"The eyes of all wait upon Thee; and Thou givest them their meat in due season. Thou openest thine hand, and satisfiest the desire of every living thing"* (KJV).

**280. Do good to all, but start your giving within the family of believers.**

*"As we have opportunity, let us do good to all people, especially to those who belong to the family of believers"* (Galatians 6:10). It is great to give to secular organizations that are feeding the poor, building hospitals, searching for cures, and helping disadvantaged kids, but the first priority for our giving should be the church.

**281. If you do not plant any seed, you will never receive a harvest.**

A seed in your hand will never produce. Mike Murdock says, "If you sow no seed, you schedule a season of lack."

An old farmer was sitting on his front porch when a neighbor dropped by to talk about the planting. He asked the farmer, "How's your wheat doing?"

"Well, I decided not to plant wheat this season because it's possible we will get a drought and it won't grow," explained the farmer.

"How's the corn doing then?" inquired the neighbor.

"I was scared that it might start raining more than usual and the corn would rot in the field, so I didn't plant any."

"What about the cotton?" came a third question.

"No cotton either, the boll weevils might eat it. This year I'm playing it safe."

In the natural realm it is risky to sow seed because it is possible you will not receive a harvest, but the biggest risk is not sowing seed because then you are guaranteed not to have a harvest.

# <u>Secrets of the Seed</u>
# From Ephesians

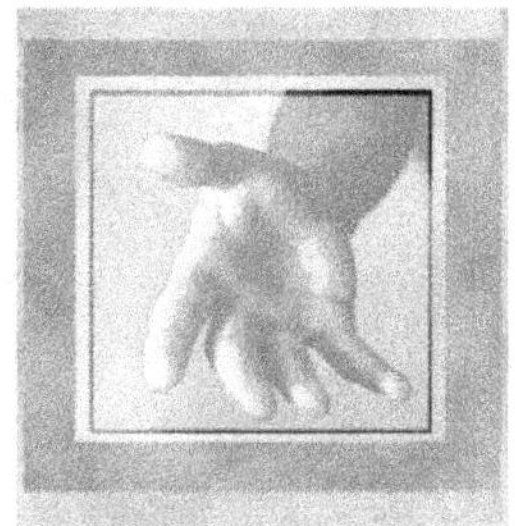

**282. God promises a bigger harvest than you can imagine.**

*"Now to Him who is able to do immeasurably more than all we ask or imagine, according to His power that is at work within us"* (Ephesians 3:20). Start thinking bigger. The bigger we think, the bigger God will act.

**283. We work so we can be a blessing to those around us.**

Robb Thompson points out that the reason people in the world work is because they are hungry. *"The laborer's appetite works for him; his hunger drives him on"* (Proverbs 16:26). But the reason believers work is to be able to bless someone else. *"He who has been stealing must steal no longer, but must work, doing something useful with his own hands, <u>that he may have something to share with those in need</u>"* (Ephesians 4:28).

**284. Prosperity is God's will for your life.**

Before you can believe for prosperity you must know God's

financial will for your life. *"Therefore do not be foolish, but understand what the Lord's will is"* (Ephesians 5:17). In some areas of life we need to pray in order to discover God's specific will for a situation. For example, we should pray about who we are supposed to marry, where we should live, and what church to go to, etc. But if God's will concerning a certain subject is revealed in God's word then there is no need to pray about it because God has already made His position clear.

God's word reveals God's will. If you can find a promise of God in the Bible that applies to your situation, you can know God's will for your life. Throughout this book are hundreds of God's promises. Just find one concerning your situation and start believing it.

**286. The word in your heart waters the seed in your garden.**

How do you water your seed? *"...with water through the word..."* (Ephesians 5:26).

# Secrets of the Seed From Philippians

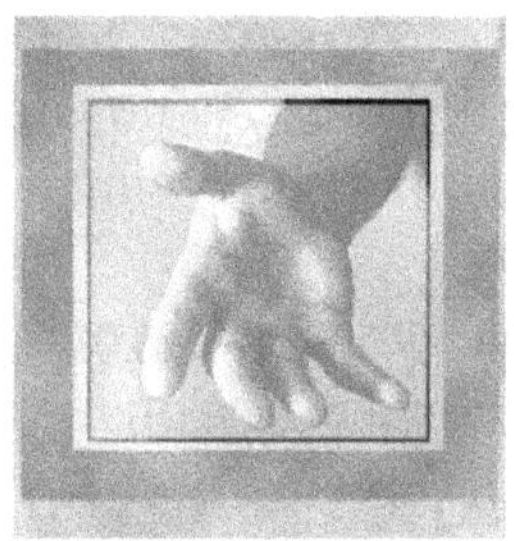

**287. God, not wealth, is all you ever really need.**

*"I am not saying this because I am in need, for I have learned to be content whatever the circumstances. I know what it is to be in need, and I know what it is to have plenty. I have learned the secret of being content in any and every situation, whether well fed or hungry, whether living in plenty or in want. I can do everything through Him who gives me strength"* (Philippians 4:11-13).

**288. Every minister needs partners.**

*"Yet it was good of you to share in my troubles"* (Philippians 4:14). Every minister who is legitimately meeting needs has someone who is called to help him or her.

**289. Your giving sets you apart from the crowd and makes you significant in someone's life.**

*"Moreover, as you Philippians know, in the early days of your acquaintance with the gospel, when I set out from Macedonia,*

*not one church shared with me in the matter of giving and receiving, except you only; for even when I was in Thessalonica, you sent me aid again and again when I was in need"* (Philippians 4:15-16).

**290. Giving and receiving go hand in hand.**

"*...Giving and receiving...*" (Philippians 4:15). If churches talk about giving without talking about receiving, they are missing half of God's equation. Some religious leaders steal from God's people by condemning receiving. They literally rob believers of expectation. This takes all the joy out of giving. It is much easier to be a joyful giver when you know you will be a receiver.

It would be foolish for a farmer to plant seed if there is no hope for a harvest. Why would a farmer work hard plowing the ground and planting his seed if there was never any harvest? No, a farmer sows with the expectation of receiving a harvest. The harvest is his motivation for planting.

Would a businessman ever invest in a business which has zero chance of giving him a return on his money? No, a businessman invests where there is the greatest probability for dividends. The profit is his motivation for investing.

God does not ask the believer to go against the wisdom of the farmer and the businessman. God asks us to give, but He promises to give back to us. Our expectation for receiving is our motivation for giving.

It is not unnatural to expect something in return for what you give. Are you surprised when a fast food restaurant gives you a hamburger in return for your money? Are you astonished when your employer gives you a paycheck in exchange for two weeks worth of work? Does it confuse you when a vending machine gives you a soda for your coin? Should you be shocked that God will give you a harvest on the seeds you plant?

Do we "give" to "get?" Yes! Jesus clearly said, "Give and it will be given unto you." The reason we "get" when we "give" is that our giving proves that in our "getting" we will not forget to give again.

**291. The smart seed-sower gives systematically.**

The church in Philippi gave regularly to Paul. He wrote, *"you sent me aid again and again when I was in need"* (Philippians 4:16). Regular habitual giving is one of the best spiritual habits you can develop.

Inconsistent giving produces inconsistent harvests. A farmer who only sows once every ten years cannot expect to receive a harvest every year. If your needs are being met haphazardly, then it might be because your giving has been haphazard.

**292. God is not trying to get something from you, He is trying to get something to you.**

*"Not that I am looking for a gift, but I am looking for what may be credited to your account"* (Philippians 4:17). What is the balance in your heavenly bank account?

**293. Your money smells good in God's nostrils.**

*"I have received full payment and even more; I am amply supplied, now that I have received from Epaphroditus the gifts you sent. They are a fragrant offering, an acceptable sacrifice, pleasing to God"* (Philippians 4:18). At one of my crusades in the Dominican Republic, we received an offering for the local pastors. Over 30,000 people were present and many of them gave generously especially considering their impoverished circumstances. Afterwards, my team of teenagers helped to count the money. The most common denomination of bill was a one paso note worth about five cents. Thousands of these crumpled bills were wet from the sweat of the people who had given. Frankly, the pile of money smelled horrible. The phrase "filthy stinking lucre" came to my mind, but then I realized that in God's nostrils, the money was a sweet smelling offering sitting on the altar in front of His throne.

**294. Giving is an act of worship.**

In the Old Testament every worshiper who came to the temple was required to give something to God. Paul tells the Philippian church their gift to him is *"an acceptable sacrifice, pleasing to God."* (Philippians 4:18).

**295. Giving moves God's blessings from the category of what <u>He is able</u> to do for you to the category of what <u>He will do</u> for you.**

In 2 Corinthians 9:8, Paul tells the Corinthian church, *"<u>God is able</u> to make all grace abound to you, so that in all things at all times, having all that you need, you will abound in every good work."* But later, Paul tells the Philippian church, *"<u>My God will</u> meet all your needs according to His glorious riches in Christ Jesus"* (Philippians 4:19). How do we move from the description of what God is able to do on our behalf to the promise that He will do something on our behalf?

The answer to this question lies in the area of our giving. In 2 Corinthians, Paul asks the church to give and he essentially says "If you give, God is able to bless you." But in Philippians the situation is different. The church has faithfully supported Paul for a long time and he is thanking them for their generosity. He basically says, "Because you have given, God will bless you."

So, what does this truth mean for you? Your giving will move God's blessings from the category of what He is able to do for you to the category of what He will (positively, without a shadow of a doubt) do for you.

<u>What is God able to do for you?</u>

* He is able to make you prosperous.
* He is able to heal you.
* He is able to bring peace to your family.
* He is able to give you all you need with enough left over to be a blessing to those around you.

<u>What will God do for you?</u>

* That is determined by your giving.

# Secrets of the Seed From Paul

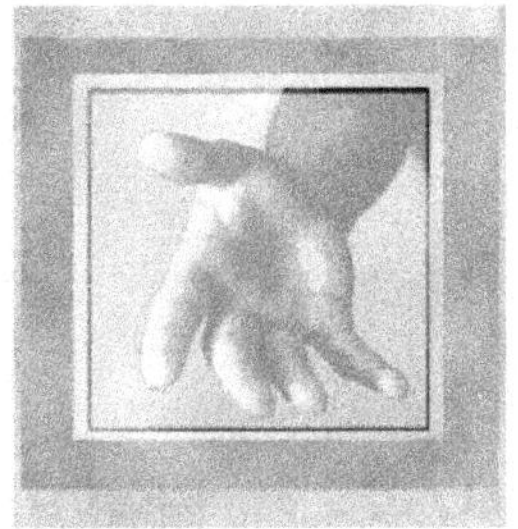

**296. Giving is not a substitute for labor; it is a multiplier of labor.**

God is not going to bless you if you are not going to work. Paul said, *"If a man will not work, he shall not eat"* (2 Thessalonians 3:10). Sowing seed does not make up for laziness on the job, rebellion toward your boss, or lying. One good deed does not cancel out previous bad deeds.

*"Lazy hands make a man poor, but diligent hands bring wealth"* (Proverbs 10:4). Slack hands bring you to ruin, but diligent hands cause you to prosper. *"The LORD will...bless all the work of your hands..."* (Deuteronomy 28:12). If you need some money, it is not enough to just wish for it, find a job. I'm reminded of the baker who hung a help wanted sign outside his bakery which said, "Need Dough? Knead Dough!"

Get-rich-quick schemes do not work. Be diligent instead of looking for a shortcut. *"All hard work brings a profit, but mere talk leads only to poverty"* (Proverbs 14:23). "*Dishonest money dwindles away, but he who gathers money little by little makes it grow"*

(Proverbs 13:11).

If you are faithful to work hard God will see that your efforts are multiplied. *"The plans of the diligent lead to profit as surely as haste leads to poverty"* (Proverbs 21:5).

We need to work hard, but we also need to work smart. *"If any of you lacks wisdom, he should ask God, who gives generously to all without finding fault, and it will be given to him"* (James 1:5). God will give you creative ideas which will lead to increased productivity and finances. *"I wisdom, dwell with prudence, and find out knowledge of witty inventions"* (Proverbs 8:12 KJV).

**297. If you are too poor to take care of your family, you are out of God's will just as much as an unsaved person is out of God's will for his life.**

*"If anyone does not provide for his relatives, and especially for his immediate family, he has denied the faith and is worse than an unbeliever"* (1 Timothy 5:8).

**298. Do you have money or does money have you?**

*"...godliness with contentment is great gain. For we brought nothing into the world, and we can take nothing out of it. But if we have food and clothing, we will be content with that. People who want to get rich fall into temptation and a trap and into many foolish and harmful desires that plunge men into ruin and destruction"* (1 Timothy 6:6-9).

**299. When you die you can take nothing with you.**

A colleague of a famous film producer tried to persuade him to give money to a charity. The man reasoned, "You can't take it with you when you go."

"If I can't take it with me," retorted the producer, "I won't go."

This is a funny story, but the truth is that everyone will die eventually (Hebrews 9:27). When we die, we can take nothing with us. *"For we brought nothing into the world, and we can take nothing out of it"* (1 Timothy 6:7). Every baby is born naked and penniless. Every person who dies takes nothing into the afterlife. You arrived with nothing and you will leave with nothing. *"Naked a man comes from his mother's womb, and as he comes, so he departs. He takes nothing from his labor that he can carry in his hand"* (Ecclesiastes 5:15).

There is a joke about a man who wanted to take his money with him when he died. He asked his doctor, his pastor, and his lawyer to come into his sickroom. He handed each of them a package of $100 bills and asked them to make sure the money was in his coffin when he died. When the funeral arrived, the three men placed the packages in the dead man's hands right before he was lowered into the grave.

As they walked away, the doctor made a confession, "Guys, I feel bad, I replaced the money in the packet with old newspapers and used it to build a new wing on the hospital."

At this news, the pastor looked ashamed and admitted, "I did the same thing and sent the money to some missionaries."

The lawyer looked indignant and angry. "How dare you take his money! He entrusted it to you and asked you to bury it with him. I want you to know that I was absolutely honest. I deposited his money in my bank account and wrote him a check for the entire amount."

**300. Money is not evil.**

*"For the love of money is a root of all kinds of evil. Some people, eager for money, have wandered from the faith and pierced themselves with many griefs"* (1 Timothy 6:10).

It is the love of money that is the root of all evil, not money itself. Here are some thoughts about money:

* Money is a medium of exchange for goods and services.

In God's economy faith is the medium of exchange. The good news is we can use faith to move money into our hands. The exchange rate is one mustard seed amount of faith to move an entire mountain of debt.

* Money is time represented in the form of paper.

Money is a symbol for your sweat, creativity, diligence, and time. You exchange your time for money. God does not really want your money, He wants you. Time spent is proof of love. Giving money represents the time you put into earning that money.

* Money is a tool.

Money is not inherently good or evil. It is neutral. It takes on the character of the person who holds it. Money can be a tool used for good or a tool used for evil.

* Money is a spiritual force.

Money makes people move on earth. Equally important to understand is that it can also make demons and angels move in the supernatural realm. When we give in an offering, it changes heaven's priorities.

* Money is the answer to life's problems.

Solomon said, *"Money is the answer for everything"* (Ecclesiastes 10:19). We need money to buy food, to provide a place to live, to purchase a car, and to communicate the gospel. Money is actually the root of much good!

* Money is sexy.

Why would a young woman marry a rich old man? Money attracts.

* Money is power.

Those with money control those without money. Those with power attract those with money.

* Money can be commanded.

Leroy Thompson confesses, "Money cometh to me now." He speaks wealth into his life. We can do the same.

* Money is governed by economic laws.

If you can learn the laws of money, you will be rich. Money must be taken seriously. Those who play with money lose money. Someone who is serious about money is always available and willing to take it from the playful. The fool and his money are soon parted.

* Money can be attracted.

If you have money, you can use it to attract more money. If

you have passion, you can attract resources to your dream. If you have a good idea, you can attract investors.

<u>* Money is a side effect of success.</u>

Tim Redmond says, "Accumulation of money should be a result not a pursuit. Once you start chasing money, it becomes mammon. Money is a great follower but a horrible leader. Wealth is a creation of God, money is a creation of man. Wealth is a creation of value for someone else."

<u>* Money is a reward for solving problems.</u>

Mike Murdock says, "Money is a reward for solving someone's problems." Why do lawyers and trash collectors get paid different amounts of money? They solve different problems. If you do not have enough money, it is because you are not solving a big enough problem.

**301. Put your trust in God, not in riches.**

*"Command those who are rich in this present world not to be arrogant nor to put their hope in wealth, which is so uncertain, but to put their hope in God, who richly provides us with everything for our enjoyment"* (1 Timothy 6:17).

**302. Give generously.**

*"Command them to do good, to be rich in good deeds, and to <u>be generous</u> and willing to share. In this way they will lay up treasure for themselves as a firm foundation for the coming age, so that they may take hold of the life that is truly life"* (1 Timothy 6:18-19).

# <u>Secrets of the Seed</u> From Hebrews, James, Peter, and John

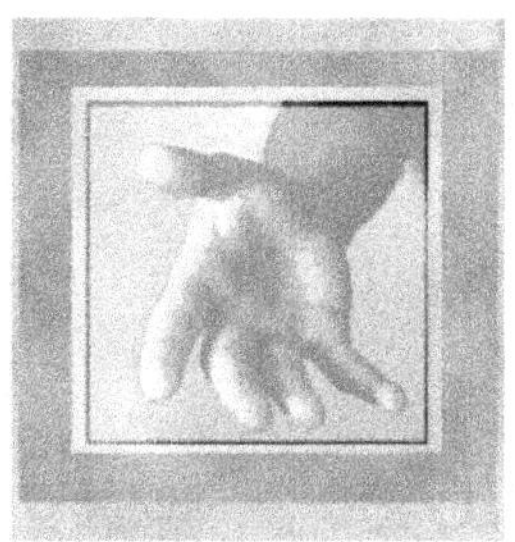

**303. The seed of discipline grows a harvest of righteousness and peace.**

*"No discipline seems pleasant at the time, but painful. Later on, however, it produces a harvest of righteousness and peace for those who have been trained by it"* (Hebrews 12:11).

**304. Everything that is good in life comes from God.**

*"Every good and perfect gift is from above, coming down from the Father of the heavenly lights..."* (James 1:17).

**305. Selfish seed produces an evil harvest, but those who sow peace reap a right relationship with God.**

*"For where you have envy and selfish ambition, there you find disorder and every evil practice...peacemakers who sow in peace raise a harvest of righteousness"* (James 3:16-18).

**306. The time of waiting between sowing and reaping proves our trust in God.**

*"Be patient, then, brothers, until the Lord's coming. See how the farmer waits for the land to yield its valuable crop and how patient he is for the autumn and spring rains"* (James 5:7). Mike Murdock explains, "Mushrooms spring up overnight, grain grows in a few months, an oak tree requires years of waiting. The size of your harvest determines the length of your wait."

**307. Earthly seed dies but the seed of God's word is eternal.**

*"For you have been born again, not of perishable seed, but of imperishable, through the living and enduring word of God"* (1 Peter 1:23).

**308. The greatest accomplishments of mankind are nothing but temporary harvests which will fade away.**

*"All men are like grass, and all their glory is like the flowers of the field; the grass withers and the flowers fall, but the word of the Lord stands forever"* (1 Peter 1:24-25).

**309. You are chosen for wealth because you are royalty.**

*"You are a chosen people, a royal priesthood..."* (1 Peter 2:9). God has chosen you for success, peace, joy, divine health, prosperity, and abundant blessings. All this is your birthright as a king.

**310. Everything we have comes from God.**

*"His divine power has given us everything we need for life..."* (2 Peter 1:3). Through God's provision, we have everything we need in life.

**311. Health and wealth are God's will for your life.**

*"Beloved, I wish above all things that thou mayest prosper and be in health, even as thy soul prospereth"* (3 John 1:2 KJV).

**312. For every man of God with a vision there are many in the church called to be provisionaries.**

*"Unto Him that loved us...And hath made us kings and priests*

*unto God"* (Revelation 1:5-6 KJV). Charles Nieman teaches about the relationship between kings and priests. The purpose of this relationship is to build God's kingdom. According to him, the primary purpose of priests (those in full-time ministry) is to provide "vision." The purpose of kings (those in the church who are called to work in the secular realm) is to provide "provision for the vision." The reason the Church is lacking is because too many kings are trying to fulfill the duties of the priests (like Saul did when he offered a sacrifice instead of waiting for Samuel) instead of walking in their God-given anointing for earning money.

## How God Broke the Spirit of Stinginess in Me

I was sitting in the second row of a pastor's conference. For eight hours, the man of God had poured into our lives. I could not take notes fast enough because every word he spoke was dripping with wisdom. Finally he shared about purchasing a new building. He asked the ministers in the room to give toward the worthy project.

Before I arrived that morning, I had already decided not to give. I had paid to attend the conference and I figured that was enough. I knew the minister was really good at taking up offerings so I had my best defenses up. This was really a stingy, miserly, Ebenezer Scrooge attitude because I wanted to receive the value of his wisdom without giving anything in return. Looking back I am astounded at the foolishness of my position, because I even desired to have a relationship with the minister without actually giving anything of value to him.

As the minister continued to share his vision, the Holy Spirit started prompting me to give. Reluctantly I gave in and decided to give $50. The minister asked everyone who wanted to give $1,000 to come to the front of the room. To my surprise 80% of the ministers went forward. I was left sitting in my seat with about fifteen other people. I promised myself that if he asked for a lower amount, I would go forward. Instead he asked for those who wanted to pledge $7,000 to come stand on the stage. Eight people went up. Finally he asked who wanted to give $25,000. Two people went up. The seats where I was sitting looked awfully empty.

I felt manipulated. I did not want to give. I was mad at God and I was mad at the minister. I was mad at all the other ministers in the room who went up front because their generosity made my stinginess look bad.

In the midst of my anger, God disciplined me. He asked me a question, "Daniel, do you believe in seedtime and harvest or not?"

It hit me like a ton of bricks. I was already working on this book. I was asking my partners to give generously to me. Spiritually I agreed with the principles of sowing and reaping, but intellectually I still struggled with wanting to hold on to my money.

God told me to give $1,000. I reminded God that I did not have $1,000 to give. God told me to give what I could and to pledge to give the rest within one year. God prompted me to immediately give $520 I was saving to buy a couch for my living room. I argued with God's instruction. He gently reminded me that all my money had come from Him anyway.

I lost the argument. I made out a check and planted the seed. I felt like a farmer pulling himself out of bed early in the morning to go plow the fields. He does not like doing it but he knows the plowing has to be done.

An hour later I started to feel good about giving. The next three months God tremendously blessed me. I received tens of thousands of dollars in donations towards one of my crusades.

I was able to complete my pledge. On the same day I finished giving, God opened up a door of tremendous favor with the same minister. He ordered 300 copies of my *Healing Power* book!

At that time, it was the biggest book order I had ever received. I was so excited. God tripled my original seed in three months. Any businessman in the world would love an investment that triples his money in three months.

Let us look at the question God asked me. "Daniel, do you believe in seedtime and harvest or not?" You see, I thought I believed it, but when the rubber hit the road I was not willing to demonstrate my belief. Many Christians have the same attitude. They say they believe what the Bible says, but when it comes to actually doing something they sit back with their arms folded.

*"But be ye doers of the word, and not hearers only, deceiving your own selves"* (James 1:22 KJV). If you nod your head at what the preacher is saying, but keep your hands in

your pockets when it comes time to do something, you are just deceiving yourself. You are not really a believer, you are just pretending to be a believer. You are playing games with God and lying to yourself. According to Robb Thompson, the worst liars are those who lie to themselves.

You see, if you truly believe in seedtime and harvest you would always be sowing seed. You would be reaping a continual harvest.

# Secrets of the Seed From the Smart Seed-Sower

**313. The smart seed-sower never gets jealous when someone else reaps a harvest.**

Do not get jealous when someone else gets blessed. Get excited. If God can do it for someone else, He can do it for you. Heaven is not bankrupt just because someone else received a blessing. Heaven's barrel has no bottom. Heaven's wells do not run dry. Let their blessing build your faith.

**314. The smart seed-sower knows that sowing can make up for personal weakness.**

Everyone has weaknesses. Each person has annoying habits and traits which could lead to failure. But being known as a giver will compensate for many flaws. Instead of tolerating your existence, people will celebrate your presence. If you are a giver, everyone will be happy to see you coming.

**315. The smart seed-sower understands that harvests (both good and bad) are the result of seeds sown.**

Everything that happens to you in life is the result of a seed sown. You might not even remember the seeds you sowed years ago which are producing the results you are experiencing today. If you do not like the life you are living, then it is time for you to plant some new seeds.

**316. The smart seed-sower keeps his eyes on the harvest.**

Look at your harvest. Don't look at what your seed will cost you. Look at what your harvest will bring you.

**317. Giving demonstrates thankfulness for what God has done in the past.**

Your giving shows God you are grateful for all He has done for you in the past. You are acknowledging that everything you own was His first and the only reason you have it is because He trusts you with it.

**318. Giving demonstrates trust for what God is going to do in the future.**

When I take teenagers on short-term mission trips we do team-building exercises. One of these involves asking a teen to fall backwards off an elevated step into the arms of the team members. This exercise is designed to build trust.

If you are worried about the future, you tend to hoard as much as you can because of the uncertainties of tomorrow. Giving can feel like you are falling backwards hoping that God will catch you. But, your giving proves to God that you trust Him for your future.

**319. Giving prepares your future.**

Your future is a blank canvas. The seeds you plant today travel into your future and paint a picture of prosperity for you to enjoy. Giving unlocks your destiny.

**320. Giving keeps you humble.**

Giving requires great humility. When you give you are saying, "I think this money is worth more in the hands of my spiritual mentor than it is in my hands." You acknowledge that the seed is worth more in the ground than it is in your stomach.

**321. Giving opens the door for miracles.**

You do not exchange money for a miracle. You sow for a miracle. Mike Murdock points out, "You cannot buy a miracle, but you can sow for a miracle." You see, money is a medium of exchange. Buying is an exchange of something valuable for something of equal value. But there is nothing equal about sowing and reaping. You sow a little and get a lot. The only way you can ever hope for a miracle is through the infinite power of multiplication found within the tiny seed.

In Acts 8, Peter and John were praying for people to receive the Holy Spirit. Simon the sorcerer offered them money and said, "Give me this ability so that everyone on whom I lay my hands may receive the Holy Spirit." Peter rebuked him, "May your money perish with you, because you thought you could buy the gift of God with money! You have no part or share in this ministry, because your heart is not right before God. Repent of this wickedness and pray to the Lord. Perhaps He will forgive you for having such a thought in your heart. For I see that you are full of bitterness and captive to sin."

Simon made the mistake of thinking he could buy a blessing. You cannot buy a miracle because you cannot afford a miracle. They are priceless. How can you buy something that is infinitely valuable? There is no price tag on miracles.

* You can buy medicine, but how can you buy healing?
* You can buy a wedding ring, but how can you buy a peaceful marriage?
* You can buy a car with safety features, but how can you buy safety?
* You can buy a house, but how can you buy a happy home?

You cannot buy a miracle, but you can sow a seed which will produce a miracle harvest!

**322. Giving is a sacrifice.**

In the world's system no one can ever afford to give. If you can afford to give what you are giving, you are not giving enough. C.S. Lewis said, "I do not believe one can settle how much we ought to give. I am afraid the only safe rule is to give more than we can spare." If your giving does not move you, then it does not move God.

**323. Giving moves God's blessings from His hand to your hand.**

Mike Murdock explains, "Everything in your hand is a seed. Everything in God's hand is a harvest. When you release what is in your hand, God releases what is in His hand. Your giving moves God's blessings from His hand into your hand."

**324. Develop a rhythm of giving.**

Billy Joe Daugherty says, "The provision for seedtime is found in the harvest, and provision for the harvest is found in the seedtime. There is a cycle where one provides for the other. Out of the harvest comes the seed, and out of the seedtime comes a harvest." We should make giving a habit. Give, reap a harvest, give again, reap a bigger harvest.

# Facts about the Seed

**325. A seed is anything you plant to get a harvest.**

**326. A harvest is anything a seed produces.**

**327. God established the process of seedtime and harvest at the beginning of time.**

**328. The way a seed grows reveals an integral, eternal, immutable, aspect of God's character.**

**329. Seedtime and harvest will never cease.**

**330. The seeds you sow determine the harvests you grow.**

**331. Sowing is not an euphemism for giving, it is a spiritual description of giving.**

**332. Your income is dependent on what you do with your outgo.**

**333. God gives us harvests, not just to raise our standard of living, but to raise our standard of giving.**

**334. Your life is the most significant seed you can sow.**

**335. A seed can satisfy your hunger today, or produce a harvest tomorrow; the same seed cannot do both.**

**336. The time of your greatest need should be the time you plant your greatest seed.**

**337. If you are not willing to give God everything, you don't have the right to ask God for anything.**

**338. If you doubt, you'll do without. If you believe, you will receive.**

# Facts about How God Interacts with Seeds

**339. When you talk to God about a need, He talks to you about a seed.**

**340. God is only obligated to bring a harvest on seed He directed you to plant.**

**341. Every time God gives us a chance to sow seed, He is giving us the option to multiply our income.**

**342. God is responsible for multiplying the seed and bringing increase, but you are responsible for sowing the seed.**

**343. If God can get it <u>through</u> you, then He will get it <u>to</u> you.**

**345. God does not ask you for what you do not have, He asks for what you want to hold on to.**

# Facts about the Harvest

**346. You must plant a seed before you can expect a harvest.**

**347. You always reap what you sow.**

**348. You always reap more than you sow, the harvest is always bigger than the seed.**

**349. You always reap in a different season.**

**350. You always reap in an appointed season.**

**351. You only reap what you plant so only plant what you want to reap.**

**352. The size of your harvest depends on the size of your seed.**

**353. Harvest time should be all-the-time.**

**354. Don't criticize a man's harvest unless you know the size of his seed.**

# More Thoughts about the Seed

**355. The world works on Supply and Demand. The kingdom of God works on Demand and Supply.** If we create the demand, God has to supply. If you are obedient to God, you place a demand on God and He supplies.

**356. Some people are waiting for a ship to come in and they have never sent a ship out.** You have to sow some seed before you can ever reap a harvest.

**357. Your seed is asleep. You must wake it up by planting it.**

**358. Your seed is a photograph of your future.**

**359. Lots of people want to give God the credit but they don't want to give him the cash.**

**360. Prosperity is not about possessions, but about priorities. It's not about money but about obedience.**

**361. God's blessing on your life is a matter of choice, not chance.**

**362. Life is God's gift to you, but what you do with your life is your gift to God.**

**363. Expectation is the key to unlocking miracles in your life.** People say, "I don't like to give expecting to get something from God." Did you expect to get salvation when you gave your heart to God? When you work at your job, do you expect to receive a paycheck? Or does receiving a paycheck totally surprise you? Do you give it back to your employer and say, "Please keep this check, I did not expect you to pay me."

**364. There are four types of offerings:**

**The Deed Offering** – The pastor says, "Can you donate your time to help us do something?"

**The Need Offering** – The pastor says, "We have so many needs in our ministry. Can you give a small gift to help us keep the lights on?" This type of offering is fine for a while, but soon people get tired of meeting your needs.

**The Greed Offering** – The pastor thinks to himself, "I need a new car, watch, and house. I will take up an offering in order to get rich." The purpose of an offering is to meet the needs of the people by building their faith for a harvest, not to meet the needs of the preacher.

**The Seed Offering** – The pastor says, "When you give to God, you can expect to receive a harvest." This is the most powerful form of offering that can be given. An offering in faith believing for a specific harvest.

**365. To receive a bountiful harvest, you must sow a precious seed.**

God wants you to go from giving "the possible seed" to giving "the precious seed." The possible seed is the $20 in your pocket; the precious seed is giving a meaningful amount that stretches your faith.

On special occasions, God will often ask you for a precious seed. The precious seed is the thing you don't want to give up. God will never ask you for what you don't have but God will often ask you for something precious to you.

* Abraham's precious seed was Isaac.
* The widow's precious seed was her cake.
* God's precious seed was His only Son.

Once you release your precious seed, God will release the bountiful harvest you need.

# Our Goal?
# Every Soul!

Daniel & Jessica King

# About the Author

Daniel King and his wife Jessica met in the middle of Africa while they were both on a mission trip. They are in high demand as speakers at churches and conferences all over North America. Their passion, energy, and enthusiasm are enjoyed by audiences everywhere they go.

They are international missionary evangelists who do massive soul-winning festivals in countries around the world. Their passion for the lost has taken them to over sixty nations preaching the gospel to crowds that often exceed 50,000 people.

Daniel was called into the ministry when he was five years old and began to preach when he was six. His parents became missionaries to Mexico when he was ten. When he was fourteen he started a children's ministry that gave him the opportunity to minister in some of America's largest churches while still a teenager.

At the age of fifteen, Daniel read a book where the author encouraged young people to set a goal to earn $1,000,000. Daniel reinterpreted the message and determined to win 1,000,000 people to Christ every year.

Daniel has authored twenty-one books including his best sellers *Grace Wins, Healing Power*, *The Secret of Obed-Edom*, and *Fire Power*. His book *Welcome to the Kingdom* has been given away to over half a million new believers.

# Soul Winning Festivals

Brazil
Haiti
Pakistan
Indonesia
India
Haiti
South Africa
Colombia
Peru
Nicaragua

When Daniel King was fifteen years old, he set a goal to lead 1,000,000 people to Jesus before his 30th birthday. Instead of trying to become a millionaire, he decided to lead a million "heirs" into the kingdom of God. *"If you belong to Christ then you are heirs"* (Galatians 3:29).

After celebrating the completion of this goal, Daniel & Jessica made it their mission to go for one million souls every year.

This **Quest for Souls** is accomplished through:

* Soul Winning Festivals
* Leadership Training
* Literature Distribution
* Humanitarian Relief

Would you help us lead
people to Jesus by joining
The MillionHeir's Club?

Visit www.kingministries.com to get involved!

GET THE LATEST

## THE SECRET OF OBED-EDOM

Unlock the secret to supernatural promotion and a more intimate walk with God. Unleash amazing blessing in your life!

*$20.00*

## MOVE

What is God's will for your life? Learn how to find and fulfill your destiny.

*$10.00*

## POWER OF FASTING

Discover deeper intimacy with God and unleash the answer to your prayers.

*$10.00*

TOLL FREE: 1-877-431-4276
PO BOX 701113
TULSA, OK 74170 USA

ORDER ONLINE:
WWW.KINGMINISTRIES.COM

## The Power Series

# Healing Power

Do you need healing? This power-packed book contains 17 truths to activating your healing today!

*$20.00*

# Fire Power

Inside these pages you will learn how to CATCH the fire of God, KEEP the fire of God, and SPREAD the fire of God!

*$12.00*

# Power of the Seed

Discover the power of Seedtime & Harvest! Discover why your giving is the most important thing you will ever do!

*$20.00*

Toll Free: 1-877-431-4276
PO Box 701113
Tulsa, OK 74170 USA

Order Online:
www.KingMinistries.com

# Sow what?

If your faith has been stirred by reading this book, I encourage you to sow a seed today. When you sow, wrap your faith around your seed and expect a miracle harvest!

Would you sow a financial seed into our ministry today? We are a soul winning ministry dedicated to leading people to Jesus all over the world.

If you sow a seed into our ministry, it will produce two harvests. The first harvest will be a harvest of souls as we use the money to reach the lost. The second harvest will be a harvest of miracles in your life.

When you send me your seed, tell me what you are asking God for and I will agree with you for your miracle.


Write:
King Ministries International
PO Box 701113
Tulsa, OK 74170 USA

King Ministries Canada
PO Box 3401
Morinville, Alberta T8R 1S3 Canada

Call toll-free:
1-877-431-4276

Visit us online:
www.kingministries.com

E-Mail:
daniel@kingministries.com

www.ingramcontent.com/pod-product-compliance
Lightning Source LLC
Chambersburg PA
CBHW071435090426
42737CB00011B/1669

* 9 7 8 1 9 3 1 8 1 0 0 2 9 *